MEN-AT-ARMS SERIES

EDITOR: MARTIN WINDROW

British Battledress

1937-61

Text by BRIAN JEWELL

Colour plates by MIKE CHAPPELL

OSPREY PUBLISHING LONDON

Published in 1981 by
Osprey Publishing Ltd
59 Grosvenor Street, London W1X 9DA
© Copyright 1981 Osprey Publishing Ltd
Reprinted 1983, 1984, 1985, 1987, 1988

ISBN 0 85045 387 9

Filmset in Great Britain
Printed in Hong Kong

Author and publishers wish to acknowledge their
gratitude to all who helped with advice and
information during the preparation of this book,
notably: Dr R. A. Blease and staff, Quality
Assurance Directorate, MOD; Maj. D. I. A. Mack,
Regimental HQ, The Royal Highland Fusiliers; Lt.
Col. George Forty; Lt. Col. R. K. May, Regimental
Museum, The Border Regt. & The King's Own
Border Regt.; Maj. D. J. Machray, Regimental HQ,
QARANC; Maj. R. R. M. Parker, Corps HQ,
WRAC; Lt. Col. A. C. M. Urwick, DL, The Light
Infantry Office (Somerset); and staff of the Chemical
Defence Establishment; the National Army Museum;
the RAC Tank Museum, Bovington; the Royal
Marines Museum; the Airborne Forces Museum; the
Imperial War Museum; the Dept. of National
Defence, Canada; and Defence HQ, South Africa.

Introduction

At the end of the 1930s more than a few British Army Drill Sergeants must have suffered nightmares after the announcement of a new uniform for the British soldier. Traditional methods are sacred to such men, and their professional world was already shaken by a flood of civilians in uniform and by Mr Hoare Belisha's new barracks. Now they had to accommodate their professional standards to a uniform which resembled a mechanic's overalls, with a huge pocket on the front of the left thigh just where there ought to be a razor-edged crease, and without even any buttons which would take a shine.

It is sadly true that many who wore battledress showed a striking resemblance to an animated sack of potatoes. Those of us with long backs found it impossible to keep the two parts of the uniform together whenever we had to bend over, this manoeuvre being attended by a pinging of buttons and a rapid cooling of the area above the kidneys. But with all its faults, battledress served its purpose well. It clothed the servicemen of many nations, at war and at peace, for more than 25 years, and did so with reasonable warmth and convenience. Its influence was to be seen in the civilian world as well, in examples as diverse as Churchill's famous 'siren suit', and the Field Jacket of the American GI. Even now, more than 40 years after battledress was created, its ghost lives on in our midst in the denim jackets of the

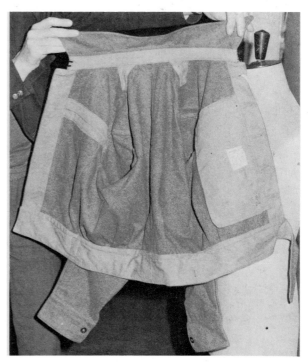

Inside and outside of the '1940 pattern' austerity BD blouse, in this case an example made by Rego Clothiers Ltd. in 1942.

fashionable young, many of whom must be unaware of the nature of the beast they have inherited.

The Arrival of Battledress

In the 1930s the War Office grew increasingly aware of the need for a new and more rational combat dress, and by 1937 the design for what would become known as 'battledress' had been evolved. Research has failed to reveal a 1937 specification for it, the first to come to light being Provisional Specification No. E/1037 of 28 October 1938. As this has no suffix to the number and makes no mention of superseding a previous specification it may perhaps be assumed to be the first relating to the new uniform. Furthermore, Army Council Instructions were strangely silent on the subject; it seems that it was not until 1940 that ACI 306 specifically mentioned it.

Arms inspection by a lieutenant and a sergeant of the King's Own Yorkshire Light Infantry near Lille during the 'Phoney War', 1939–40. The subaltern wears the SD cap, and brass shoulder strap ranking and regimental 'collar dogs' on his '1937 pattern' BD; the sergeant has regimental-pattern dark-green-on-yellow chevrons, and brass shoulder titles. (Imperial War Museum)

Although known to have been tested with some selected Regular Army units in 1937, battledress first became a general issue to the newly conscripted militia in 1938 and, judging from the early specifications, the new uniform seems to have suffered from teething troubles.

The above-mentioned specification of 28 October 1938 states that the outside breast pocket flaps shall be in line with the second buttonhole from the top. This was probably found to interfere with the wearing of the 1937 webbing equipment and braces as, in the subsequent Specification No. E/1037A of May 1939, the pockets are moved up half an inch. On 29 July 1939 E/1037B hints at a disastrous spate of split trousers by the inclusion of a clause specifying that 'seat seams shall be sewn by hand with double No. 35 thread, or by the triple lockstitch machine 6 to 7 stitches to the inch'. Another amendment of 30 December 1939 significantly underlines the increased production requirements after the outbreak of war: E/1037C allows buttons to be sewn on either by hand or by machine, whereas previously the three buttons at the back of the trouser waist, intended for the attachment of the blouse, had to be hand sewn for greater strength.

Of course, browsing among such specifications fails to give a very clear idea of the appearance of early battledress, useful though it is for dating detail variations. For the more general view we may turn to a publication named *Uniforms for the Services* which, although undated, shows the details appropriate to battledress prior to May 1939. Selected quotes from this document are as follows:

'Blouse—This is cut on very easy fitting lines. The back is cut with a raised centre back seam and the seam is raised well up on top of the shoulder. There are no sideseams. The front fastens to the neck, which is finished with a Panteen collar. The left forepart terminates directly down the centre of the front, and the fastening consists of five brass four-holed buttons concealed in a fly. There are two hooks and eyes for fastening the front of the collar on the stand. Shoulder straps of the usual width carry, in the case of officers, embroidered badges of rank. The waist section is gathered into a 2in. wide belt. Extending from the latter on the left side is a 9in. strap, which fastens with a buckle

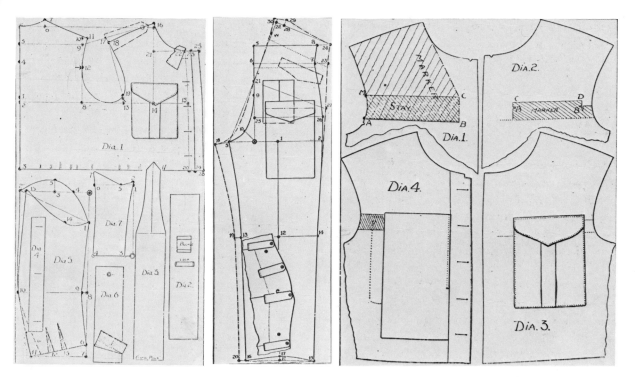

at the side waist to provide for adjustment. Patch pockets are placed on each breast, the average size of these being 6in. by 7in. with a $1\frac{1}{4}$in. box-pleat in centre. The flaps covering these pockets are made 3in. in depth at centre, tapering to 2in. at side. The pocket is closed by means of a hole and button, a concealed inner flap taking the button-hole. The sleeve is cut moderately full and finished with a 3in. wide band into which the upper part is tucked. There is a vent in the hind-arm with a button and hole in fly.

'The Trousers—These are cut moderately wide in the legs with plain bottoms. A strap is inserted in the legseam ($\frac{1}{2}$in. up) at the bottom; this is $1\frac{1}{2}$in. wide and reaches the front crease where it is attached to a button when the trousers are worn without leggings. Before the leggings are put on the strap is drawn over the front of the leg to fasten on a button placed at the sideseam for the purpose. On the left leg a deep patch pocket with a flap is placed. The position of the top of this pocket is about 9in. from the waist and $1\frac{1}{2}$in. away from the fly. The width is 7in. and depth 11in., and a flap similar to that used on the outside breast pocket is attached with a buttonhole in the lining. The flap is placed 1in. above the patch of the pocket. On the right leg is placed a patch pocket of smaller dimensions. This has a flat pleat

Cutting-out and making-up diagrams for the '37 BD, from *Uniforms of the Services*.

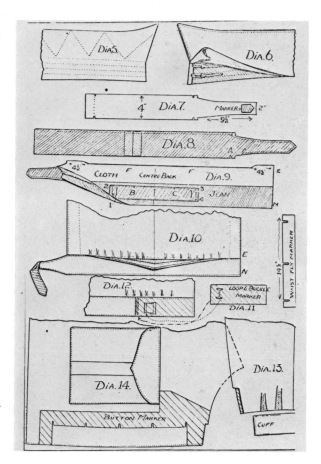

'1940 pattern' BD blouse stamped September 1944. It bears the shoulder patches of British Troops in France, 1944–45—a red shield with a blue cross; below this the red/green Pioneer Corps arm-of-service strip; and lieutenant's pips on a red backing on the shoulder straps. (Martin Windrow)

above: All buttons were pressed brass with four holes, except those on the shoulder straps and the field dressing pocket, which were plastic, usually four-hole type but sometimes metal-shanked. The collar, inside edges of the front of the blouse, two deep inside pockets, blouse belt lining and trouser pockets were all made of what was called 'Drill No. 2 Drab'—a light sandy-yellow drill material. Four belt loops, long enough to accommodate the 1937 pattern webbing belt, were provided on the trousers, buttoned at the upper ends (the loops revived on the 1949 pattern BD were buttoned at the lower ends, and only three were provided).

The author recalls having a battledress with anti-gas treatment issued from the stores of Fulwood Barracks, Preston in May 1943. It smelt terrible, and the accepted practice was to walk about in the rain in the hope of washing the impregnation out of the cloth! The impregnation gave the cloth a slightly lighter or greyer shade than those not so treated; but after prolonged wetting it was not unknown for it to turn a bilious green colour, so on balance it was probably less distressing to put up with the smell. This anti-gas treatment started early in the war, and continued until September 1945, some 13,000,000 suits of BD being so treated.

For the interest of the technically minded, the Chemical Defence Establishment states that there were two methods of impregnating cloth to give protection against vesicant vapour. The first, using activated charcoal, was thoroughly investigated, but clothing with this treatment did not become standard issue. The second method depended on a chemical reaction between the impregnant and the gas vapour whereby the latter became innocuous. For clothing intended for temperate climates the impregnant was 2, 4, dichlorophenyl-benzoyl chloroinide (AV); tropical issue clothing was treated with 2 2'44'66'NN, occachlorodiphenylurea (CC2).

A word must be said here about the 'poor relation' of the battledress, the 'Overalls, Denim', in which soldiers spent more hours, weeks, and even years than they did in the serge BD. Denims, made from a drab earth-brown jean material, were based closely on the 1937 pattern BD; they had the same number and type of outside pockets, which even retained their pleats, but the buttons

in the centre. The position of this pocket is 6in. from the top and 1in. from the fly. The size is 4½in. wide and 6in. long. [The left and right thigh pockets will hereafter be called 'map' and 'field dressing pockets' respectively.] Ordinary side pockets are inserted and there is a hip pocket with a flap at the back. This has a buttonhole in the lining to conceal the button. The brace buttons are placed inside the tops for concealment.'

Elsewhere in this numbingly tedious but useful article, which goes on to describe the method of construction, there is a further reference to the blouse sleeves: 'The original pattern had pleats at the base of the sleeve. The recent models, however, appear to be made up quite plain.' In fact, pleats did appear in many examples of later-period 1937 pattern battledress, and even in some of the 'austerity' 1940 pattern. They were always provided on Canadian- and Australian-made BD, which persisted in being of a fuller cut than BD made in the United Kingdom.

There are a few points of detail which should be added to the description given in the article quoted

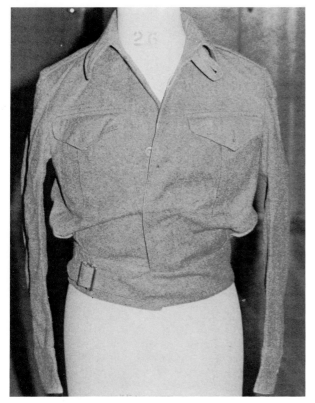
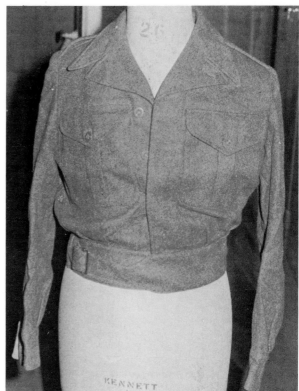

'1946 pattern' BD blouse, with tab collar; and (right) '1947 pattern', with open, 'shirt-type' collar. Made by John Hammond & Co. (1923) Ltd., and GIC, respectively.

were of the removable plastic type with a revolving metal shank, kept in place by a split-pin at the back of the cloth. This was so that buttons could be removed each time the denims were sent for washing, which was supposed to happen each week, irrespective of need, when circumstances allowed. With this constant cleaning the life of denims was short, and one was lucky to avoid gaping holes and terminally frayed collars. Naturally, one never got back from the cleaners the same suit which one had given up the week before; so the soldier's traditional battle to find a uniform which was neither too large nor too small was repeated at short intervals for months on end. Denims were an abomination, but surprisingly many soldiers were reluctant to give them up; they were often worn in battle, being much lighter than battledress for summer use.

One problem with denims was the sizing. They were designed to be worn *over* the BD to protect it when engaged in dirty chores. They were hardly ever worn in this way (except for warmth in winter); and generations of soldiers were baffled to find that the label sizes bore no relationship to the size of the wearer.

Evolution in Design

Contrary to popular belief the year 1940 did not see the disappearance of concealed buttons and pocket pleats from Army wartime battledress, although BD suits without such embellishments are referred to as '1940 pattern'. What happened in fact was that some economies were made in the cut of the cloth, resulting in a less full-fitting blouse and trousers, and in some minor features of construction.

On 6 June 1940 Specification No. U/617 superseded No. E/1037C. In this latest specification the pattern number allocated for the blouse was 114656 (replacing 11012) and for the trousers, 11457 (replacing 11326). The new pattern resembled the 1937 pattern but was of a slimmer cut; the one difference specified was the use on the field dressing pocket of 'Buttons, Vegetable Ivory, Drab with revolving shanks; or

as issued.' This was the first time that revolving-shank buttons were actually specified for BD, although earlier examples existed.

The next change came on 4 June 1941 when Specification U/617C redesignated the trouser pattern as 11721, the only difference influencing appearance being the omission of the line, 'There shall be a stay inside the hem at bottom for the buttons.' It seems that the straps for gathering the trouser bottoms into the gaiters had been declared unnecessary.

The first major step along the path of austerity came on 5 June 1942 when Specification No. U/617G replaced the earlier patterns for blouse and trousers respectively with new patterns numbered 12083 and 12084. Pocket pleats now disappeared, along with belt loops. The blouse was to be attached to the trousers by two buttons instead of three, and these were no longer hidden by a fly; indeed, only the fly in the crutch of the trousers was retained, all other buttons becoming visible. Apart from those on the shoulder straps and field dressing pocket, which had revolving shanks, all buttons were to be 'Buttons, Trousers, plastic, 4-hole CA5377'. Specification U/1076 of 15 July 1942 extended the use of these latter to the shoulder straps and field dressing pocket also. On 2 January 1943, U/1076B mentions only one inside breast pocket for the blouse: this and an earlier specification of 12 November 1942 made some changes to lining materials, but this will be described below in the section on cloth. No further specifications appear to have been issued until the introduction of the 1946 pattern blouse.

There seems to have been no regularity in the design of the BD blouse buckle, and specifications are vague. The first mention is in E/1037 of 28 October 1938: on the copy examined the word 'brass' had been crossed out from the original wording 'Buckles, prongless, brass'. The next mention, in May 1939, is simply of 'Buckles, prongless'; by 6 June 1940 the words 'or as issued' had been added. Two buckle types have been found on all examples examined during research for this book. One is pressed metal with a slide having a toothed bar to grip the drill-lined belt tab, the other a thick plated wire buckle with a slide but no serrations. Buckles were presumably made available to making-up contractors in

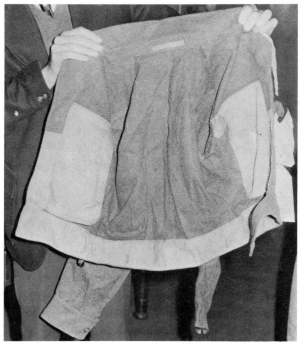

Inside and outside views of the '1949 pattern' BD blouse, with two interior pockets, an open notched collar, and pleated pockets.

batches, depending on what was being manufactured at the time.

In the last month of 1944 an Army Regulation permitted Other Ranks to wear collars and ties with BD when off duty. The prohibition of collars and ties prior to this date—officially, at least—had for a long time been a bone of contention among British soldiers, who resented the denial of a right enjoyed by members of other services. The civilians in uniform who made up the vast majority of the British Army in wartime saw no good reason why they should be forced to present an old-fashioned and unstylish appearance when walking out; the author well remembers a 'current affairs' talk held in Bradford City's football stadium in October 1943, which degenerated into a heated discussion of this point. Were British Tommies considered unequal to the 'civilized' task of knotting a tie? The hard-pressed officer giving the talk was reduced to claiming that the Army had always worn button-up collars as protection against sword thrusts. He had no satisfactory answer when asked if officers, who had worn open-collar tunics since early in the century, had sword-resistant throats. . . .

With permission to open the neck of the BD blouse came a mass of unofficial mutilations in the form of faced lapels, like those ordered by officers from their tailors for some years past. The Other Ranks were required to retain the means of closing the collar when on duty, however.

To re-cap the wartime modifications to British Army battledress:

1937	Trials of BD with Regular Army units.
1938, 28 Oct.	First available specification. BD issued to conscripted militia in this year.
1939, May	Blouse pockets raised.
1940, 6 June	Revolving-shank button for field dressing pocket.
1941, 4 June	Straps and buttons no longer fitted to trouser legs.
1942, 5 June	Introduction of austerity pattern known as '1940 pattern'. All buttons exposed apart from trouser fly. Trousers given added back curtain for extra warmth. Shoulder strap buttons to

	have revolving shank.
1942, 15 July	All buttons to be 4-hole plastic.
1943, 2 January	One inside breast pocket only.

Post-War Evolution

When the Second World War ended battledress had only been in service for eight years, and in fact had the greater part of its service still to come. It was not until the late 1960s that issue ceased, although for some years beforehand the use of BD was limited to various orders of working dress, and varied widely from unit to unit. The last specification which has come to light during the author's research for this book which covers the use of BD is UK/ISC/C 4044, dated 27 April 1967.

The 1946 pattern BD blouse was clearly the result of an attempt by authority to control the unofficial modifications which thousands of individual soldiers had been ordering from local tailors, in defiance of repeated Part I Unit Orders to the effect that uniforms must not be defaced.

From the first appearance of collars and ties among the soldiery there had been a chaotic series of modifications aimed at defeating the tendency of the drill lining material, now visible at the collar of the blouse, to become filthy after a week or two of wear. Some scrubbed it regularly,

Battledress was hardly ever issued in matching suits. These two Marines wear blouses and trousers of different dates; and note RM badge worn on Field Service caps. (Royal Marines Museum)

making the material threadbare and faded. Others bleached it with toothpaste, with spectacular results if caught in a rain shower. Increasingly, soldiers risked a charge by having local civilian tailors face the opened collar with serge, or even alter the garment completely by cutting stepped lapels. It is not recorded how many charge-sheets this practice filled up, but many unit officers adopted a fairly liberal approach. Half-hearted approval was given in some cases, with unit orders allowing these modifications so long as the collar could still be fastened closed for parade—i.e. so long as the hooks and eyes were retained, and a buttonhole made in the left front. (The latter was near-impossible with pre-1942 issues, because of the fly front.)

In 1946 an attempt at regularity produced a new pattern of blouse which, although keeping the stand-up collar, was intended to be worn open. The facings were of serge, and a button-back tab on the left standing part of the collar allowed the front to be fastened to the neck when required. Under Specification MS 197 of 2 February 1946 this blouse was also given a less austere look by having the front buttons covered by a fly, and box pleats added to the breast pockets. The pocket flaps were still button-through, however, as were the cuffs and the two waist-band buttons for attaching the 1940 pattern trousers.

In 1947 another new shape appeared. The collar of the 1947 pattern was almost identical, in fact, to that of the 1944 field blouse of the German Army. Closed, it resembled the stand collar of previous patterns, though in practice it was rarely worn this way; opened, it pressed neatly in stepped lapels. The phrase 'shirt-type' was applied to this collar, though the connection is hard to fathom. This pattern also appears to have had a fuller-cut sleeve; the example now held by the Quality Assurance Directorate has pleats at the cuff-bands, a feature not seen since early issues of 1937 pattern BD (although the Canadian and Australian pattern blouses had pleats throughout).

On 7 April 1949 Specification UK/CIC/1866C, covering 'Blouse, Battledress, 1949 Pattern' laid down the style which was to be retained for the rest of the working life of British Army BD. The collar was now an uncompromising stepped lapel with a buttonhole on the left; there were two

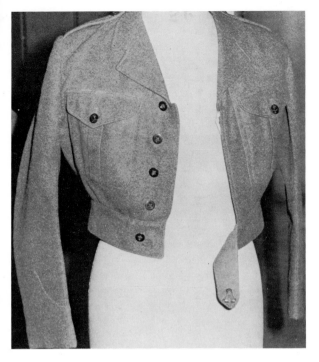

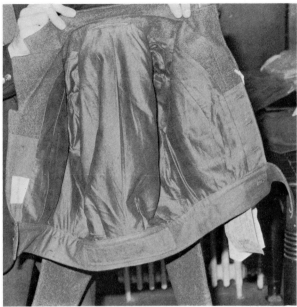

Inside and outside of WRAF 'Blouse No. 2 (Home) Dress', 1952.

inside breast pockets, and a hanger at the neck. On 9 March 1954 three buttonholes were specified in the waistband instead of two. The 1949 pattern signalled official approval for all ranks to wear collars and ties, both on and off duty. Although the face veil of camouflaged netting was normally worn as a cravat with the 1949 blouse when in the field, a tie was officially to be worn—thus negating the advantage of the collars of previous patterns, i.e. comfort when in the prone firing position.

The 1946 pattern trousers were similar to the 1942 modification of the 1940 pattern; but six more braces buttons were added. The more radical modifications of Specification UK/CIC/1843, first issued on 28 October 1947, were followed by succesive amendments; the following are extracts from UK/CIC/1843K of 2 June 1954, incorporating the last amendments found during research:

'(a) The trousers which are for wear with or without braces shall be provided with a waistband, four unseen pleats at front and two at back . . . set forward side pockets, two hip pockets with flaps, a thigh pocket with flap on the left leg [this was now at the outside of the leg instead of the front. There was no field dressing pocket] . . . three belt loops [buttoned at the lower end] . . . two hip straps and buckles, and plain bottoms.

'(c) The waistband shall be 3in. in depth on all sizes. It shall be made with the left end extended to form a shaped tab 2¼in. in length for all sizes. The end of the tab shall be provided with a metal hook to engage the bar at the right side of the waistband. . . .

'(e) Three belt loops 4in. in length . . . and one inch in width shall be provided, one at the seat seam and the other two over the pleats nearest the side pockets. . . .

'(f) The hip shall be comprised of a strap and chape ⅞th inch in width and 5in. in length. . . .

'(l) There shall be 12 brace buttons in groups of two. . . .

'(m) The two buttons on the back of the trousers, for attachment of the blouse, shall be 2½ins. from the top edge and 5½ins. from the seat seam.' (There is some inconsistency here, since the blouse specification of March 1954 mentioned three buttons.)

Basically, this so-designated 1949 pattern BD remained the standard issue. In time it came to be known as 'No. 5 Dress' in a range of fourteen Orders of Dress in the British Army, and was gradually withdrawn during the 1960s. Major D. I. A. Mack of the Royal Highland Fusiliers recalls that BD ceased to be issued to recruits at the regimental depot in the autumn of 1962, and ceased to be an item of wear for the depot staff at the same time. The following summer the men still had one suit of BD, but that was withdrawn soon afterwards. The illustrator of this book, then serving with the Gloucestershire Regiment, remembers that a single suit of BD was retained as barracks dress in the early 1960s when one suit of the new service dress was issued. The 'No. 5 Dress' trousers lasted longer than the blouse; but as late as the winter of 1970 a large batch of BD trousers and some blouses of all patterns were sent out to the regiment in Northern Ireland for wearing under the DPM camouflaged combat suit for extra warmth.

There were some attempts to make improvements to BD during its service life by testing designs which never, in the event, reached production stage; one of these was a smart version made in fine cloth.

Unofficial Modifications

The serge collar facings added by some soldiers have already been mentioned. Despite the apparently unpromising nature of the basic suit, it took only a few months of wartime service by a vast conscript army for a degree of individual styling to appear. Fashion-conscious recent ex-civilians displayed ingenuity and determination in their long battle against the dead hand of authority! Although Other Ranks were denied the benefits of the tailors and clothing coupons enjoyed by officers, there were a few tricks which could be tried. Unit tailors, an indispensable part of the establishment, had the task of fitting the 'horse collars' of the blouses to individual soldiers by making diagonal tucks above the breast pockets and putting a seam in the back of the neck. These tailors could sometimes be persuaded to exercise their skills with a rather freer hand. A reduced

Lt.Col. Hodgson, Welsh Guards, (left) and Maj.Gen. Keightley confer before the assault on Monte Cassino by 78th Division, 2 May 1944. Hodgson wears a khaki beret with the regimental leek badge embroidered in gold; '1937 pattern' BD with serge-faced lapels; bronze shoulder strap ranking of regimental pattern; white-on-black regimental title, and yellow-on-black divisional sign. Keightley has '1940 pattern' BD, with the red-banded SD cap of his rank, and gorget patches. Shoulder ranking is plain woven style, and only the divisional patch is worn on the sleeve.

number of wider pleats at the back of the blouse where it joined the waistband improved the appearance; these rear pleats were also sometimes pressed so that they fanned out in a 'wheatsheaf' shape. The hairy nap of the serge was sometimes shaved—literally, with a razor—to give a smoother finish; and most 'old soldiers' had tricks to improve the sharpness and permanence of creases in their best BD. In accordance with contemporary ideas on desirable male fashion, the shoulders of blouses were sometimes padded, and triangular gussets inserted in the trouserlegs to give a flared look. At the level of heavy engineering rather than fine tuning, most soldiers who wore BD will recall the chains (often made from lavatory chains with sheet-lead weights attached) which were temporarily 'tacked' round the inside of the lower leg to ensure a sharp, definite 'pull-down' of material over the tops of the web anklets.

Battledress of Canadian manufacture was much sought-after, being made of finer cloth and more generously cut; the same applied both to Australian BD, which was available in the 1950s in some theatres, and to some batches of BD made in America for the British Army.

Materials and Sizes

Before any item of clothing can be manufactured a prototype has to be made; in the case of the wartime British Army this was the task of the Garment Development Section, which until 1960 was based at the Royal Dockyard, Woolwich. From 1960 the GDS became part of the SCRDE, Colchester. All clothing made up at this establishment carries the letters 'GDS' on the white labels sewn to all service uniforms.

Contracting clothing manufacturers were invited to tender for producing the garments in quantity and to this end specifications were issued, pre-war by the Chief Inspector of Stores and Clothing; in 1939 the title became Chief Inspector of Clothing, and after the war, Director of Inspection of Clothing. These specifications laid down requirements relating to materials, manufacture, marking, availability of paper patterns, packing and general conditions.

RTR crewmen, c.1941–42, displaying a full range of insignia on the blouse sleeve. The black-on-khaki shoulder strap tab which replaced brass pre-war titles is worn here. At the top of the sleeve is the 'GO' patch of 8th Armoured Division, above the red/yellow Royal Armoured Corps arm-of-service strip. The white tank badge of RTR is worn on the right sleeve only, above standard rank chevrons. (Imp. War Mus.)

Materials

In the first available specification covering battledress, E/1037 of 28 October 1938, the material for the body of the garments is described as 'Serge SD No. 1 55″ Pattern No. T 90'. In June 1942 'T 90' was dropped from the specification; judging from examples examined, this implied a lighter weight cloth. The next change did not come until after the war when the material is described as 'Serge SD No. 4 56″'. ('SD' in this context stands for 'Service Dress'.) The material for ATS battledress was described as 'Serge, Saxony. 56″'; and that of Royal Navy Working Dress as 'Serge, worsted and woollen, blue, 60″. Patt. T 76'. (See below for more detail on naval and women's battledress.)

Although covered by specification, the cloth used for British Army battledress varied considerably in both weight and colour, depending on the batch from mill production. A rank of soldiers on

Commonwealth officers wearing '37 BD. (Left) Maj.Gen. Brink, commanding the South African 1st Division (yellow over green diamond) wears his ranking on khaki drill shoulder strap tabs; under the sabre-and-baton is the broad orange strip worn across the outer end of shoulder straps by all SA volunteers for overseas service. Note gorget patches. South African ranking was of British pattern. (Right) A New Zealand lieutenant-colonel displays his nation's white-on-black national title at the end of the shoulder strap ranking tab. (Imp. War Mus.)

parade was hardly ever completely uniform, and the variation extended to the colour of a single squaddie's blouse and trousers. Suits were often mixed—1937 blouses with 1940 trousers, etc.—and the differences in finish and shade were the more obvious for being seen close together.

The details covered in specifications extended to the stays for front edges and other purposes, cotton threads, hooks and eyes, buttons, and lining material. Precise making-up instructions were given, to the extent of specifying the number of stitches to the inch, the number of stitches to be used for attaching buttons, and so forth.

Sizes

Twenty standard sizes of battledress were laid down for the 1937 pattern, ranging from Extra Small (intended for men of 5ft 1in. to 5ft 2in. tall, with chest of 29in. to 30in. and waist of 27in. to 30in.) to Size No. 18 (for men of 6ft to 6ft 2in. tall,

with chest of 43in. to 44in. and waist of 38in. to 39in.). In January 1942 two additional small sizes were included: No. 01 for men of 4ft 3in. to 4ft 7in., and No. 02 for men of 4ft 8in. to 5ft tall. After the war, for the 1949 battledress, a further seven intermediate sizes were introduced, making a total of 29 fittings. Special Gurkha troops' sizes were added to post-war schedules. Note that sizes were laid down in series of three, for slim, 'normal' and corpulent soldiers of the same height range. Thus the next fitting up for a man who outgrew Size 7 was Size 10. This system led to a certain amount of confusion among quartermasters and contributed to the outrageous mis-fitting of some issue early in the war.

When battledress was introduced for women in September 1941 there were 20 sizes listed in the schedule, but this seems to have been a gross over-estimate of requirements, as the list was reduced to a mere six sizes the following month.

When wartime austerity was forgotten a greater range of sizes was available; for instance, in 1963 there were no less than 36 sizes listed for Naval Cadets' Working Dress.

Marking

To quote from the 28 October 1938 specification: 'Each garment shall be fitted (in the same position as the Standard Pattern) with a stitched-on calico or linen label (if of calico the edges shall be turned in) giving the broad arrow, name of the article, the size, particulars of measurements, the name of the contractor and the month and year of delivery.' These labels were to be found inside the left breast of the blouse. Some examples of blouse labels, which may be of interest to collectors of uniforms, are as follows:

> BATTLEDRESS
> BLOUSES, 1940 Pattern
> Size No. 15
>
> Height 5ft 11ins. to 6ft 0ins.
> Breast   42ins. to 43ins.
> Waist   37ins. to 38ins.
>
> Service Tailoring Co. Ltd.
>
> 1943
> ↑
> 25747

The '25747' is in the form of a violet ink stamp; and the same method is used to apply a large '15'

to the drill material of the inside pocket below the label—this repetition of the size number is common to all examples examined. The blouse from which the above label is taken is a standard wartime type but with the collar faced with serge and tailored open in notched form, for use after 1949: it is in fact the basis of colour plate H2.

Another example examined, dated 'October 1938' at the foot of the label, had the first two lines in the form 'BATTLEDRESS/BLOUSES, SERGE'; and one dated 'June 1940' begins 'BATTLEDRESS/BLOUSES, SERGE SD'. Slight variations in lettering, position of phrases, etc. were common, and not too much should be read into them by collectors applying too rigidly archaeological an approach! A further pair of examples show typical variations:

Some well-known examples of formation shoulder patches: left to right, top to bottom: 2nd Army—white, blue cross, gold sword. 1 Corps—red, white spear. 30 Corps—black and white. 1st Armoured Div. (many variations)—black and white. 7th Armoured Div., 1944–45—black, red-brown jerboa trimmed white. 43rd (Wessex) Div.—blue, yellow dragon. 6th Guards Tank Brigade—white, gold sword over blue/red/blue diagonal. 4th Div. (post-war)—black, red disc, white division. These examples show variations of woven, embroidered and printed finish. Soldiers often bought smarter commercially-produced versions to add to the glory of their best walking-out BD! (Martin Windrow)

A piper and a subaltern leading a battalion of Gordon Highlanders into Tunisia, February 1943. The BD is worn with the Glengarry (left) and Balmoral (right) bonnets; the officer wears the blouse collar open over a shirt and tie in the usual manner. (Imp. War Mus.)

Pioneer Corps stationed in France in 1944–45. An unissued example of the same pattern bore the label:

> BATTLEDRESS
> BLOUSES, 1940 Pattern
> Size No. 16
>
> Height 6ft oins. to 6ft 2ins.
> Breast   39ins. to 40ins.
> Waist   34ins. to 35ins.
>
> WILSON, MCBRINN
> & CO., LTD.
> BELFAST
> 1945
> ↑

An example of the label in a wartime ATS woman's blouse reads:

> BLOUSE, BATTLEDRESS
> SERGE, ATS
>
> Size No. 3
>
> Height 5ft 5ins. to 5ft 6ins.
> Bust   33ins. to 36ins.
> Waist   25ins to 28ins.
>
> SMITH & CO.
> OCTOBER 1941
> ↑

A post-war Gurkha BD blouse bears a label of typical post-war arrangement:

> BLOUSE, BATTLEDRESS
> 1949 Pattern
> GURKHA TROOPS
> Size   G 10
>
> Height 5′5″ to 5′6″
> Breast 33ins. to 34ins.
> Waist 28ins. to 29ins.
> J. Hammond & Co, (1923) Ltd.
> ↑
> 1954

> BATTLEDRESS
> BLOUSE, 1940 Pattern
> ———
> Size No. 10
>
> Height 5ft 9ins. to 5ft 10ins.
> Breast   36ins. to 37ins.
> Waist   31ins. to 32ins.
>
> John Hammond & Co. (1923) Ltd.
>
> 1944
> ↑
> Sept. 1944

The 'Sept. 1944' is the familiar violet ink stamp, and a large '10' is similarly stamped on the pocket material below the label. This label is from an absolutely standard and unaltered wartime blouse bearing the insignia of a 1st Lieutenant of the

At this late stage it is a practical impossibility to list all the manufacturers who supplied finished battledress garments. The following are some of the names that have been found in examples examined, apart from those already quoted; all appear in khaki BD unless otherwise indicated:

Black & Co. (Clothiers) Ltd—on 1951 Civil
    Defence BD
B. Bloom Ltd
J. Compton Sons & Webb Ltd—on 1965 WRAF
    No. 2 Dress
D. Denham (1933) Ltd—on 1944 BD
M. Doniger Ltd—on 1962 Civil Defence BD
H. Edgard & Sons Ltd
Gerrish Ames & Simpkins Ltd—on 1943 and
    1946 breeches
G. I. C.—on 1947 BD
D. Gurteen & Sons Ltd—on 1945 BD
H. Hepworths Ltd
Milns Cartwright & Reynolds—on 1949 RAF
    No. 2 Dress
Modern Mantles—on 1951 Civil Defence BD
    skirts
Prices Tailors Ltd
The Rego Clothiers Ltd—on 1940 and 1942 BD

Departures from Basic

For most British Army Other Ranks of the Second World War the battledress was the universal uniform for parade, walking-out, working and fighting. Army officers, and all ranks of the other Services, had alternative uniforms, and tended to use BD as a working-dress alternative to their jacketed service dress.

The Royal Navy
The Admiralty was slow to adopt battledress and, when it was used, its main function was as a working dress on land-based stations. The growth of Combined Operations brought many sailors ashore in combat situations as the war progressed, and BD was issued for this type of duty. For most of the war the issue was standard Army khaki, worn with arc-shaped white-on-dark-blue 'Royal Navy' shoulder titles and with naval badges of rank. Officers wore their ranking on the shoulders,

either in the form of slip-over tabs on the shoulder straps bearing their gold cuff ranking, or as stiff dark blue shoulder boards. Navy blue battledress was approved in October 1943, but the first official mention which the author has been able to locate comes from an Appendix to the Navy List, December 1944, under the section entitled 'Naval Uniforms (Officers) 6A Working Dress Blouse':

'*For all Officers*—Navy serge, with step collar; single-breasted with three gilt buttons (size 1) down the front and one plain button under the right lapel. Two outside breast pockets with flaps, the flaps being $\frac{1}{2}$ inch above the second buttonhole from the top; each breast pocket measures $6\frac{1}{2}$

Well-known shot of the RSM of the Irish Guards battalion in Guards Armoured Division, with one of his crewmen, wearing an extraordinary tank crew outfit during training in the UK: it never reached front-line service! The BD blouses bear white-on-green regimental shoulder titles; the RSM has his large, fully-coloured warrant badge of the Royal Arms on the upper sleeves, and the Guardsman's left forearm displays Signals qualification flags in white and blue above a wreathed specialist's 'trade badge' above a Good Conduct chevron. (Imp. War Mus.)

inches in depth and 6 inches in width and fastens with a uniform gilt button (size 3). Body pleated with twelve pleats; belt fitted with a buttonhole to fasten to one of three plain buttons. Sleeves with plain cuffs to fasten with a plain button, fly type. The shoulders fitted with shoulder straps, except for midshipmen. *For Midshipmen, Midshipmen (E) and Paymaster Midshipmen*—On each side of the collar a white turnback of 2 inches, with a notched hole of white twist $1\frac{1}{2}$ inches long, and a corresponding button.'

The pocket flaps were of tapered—i.e. Army—shape. Photographs show pockets with and without pleats, and pockets closed with plain black plastic buttons; and blouses with the waistband

General Montgomery inspecting airborne troops, 1944. He seems to have substituted the maroon airborne beret, with Parachute Regt. and rank badges, for his usual black RAC headgear. The faced, tailored '1937 pattern' BD blouse bears metal shoulder ranking, and the patch of 21st Army Group: red shield, blue cross, yellow crossed swords. (Imp. War Mus.)

fastened with Army-type prongless buckles as well as the specified buttons. A photo of a beachmaster taken in January 1943 shows dark blue BD trousers with Army-style leg pockets, but the author has not located official mention of these. Other photos certainly show the dark blue blouse worn in conjunction with normal naval trousers.

The Royal Marines used both khaki and, later, dark blue BD during the war. The first issue of the blue type was to landing craft personnel during 1943, Royal Marines Ships detachments receiving it somewhat later. The straight red-on-dark-blue 'Royal Marines' shoulder title was normally worn. Photos show some use of the blue BD blouse with the RM service dress trousers, dark blue with a red seam welt.

Post-war use of BD by the Royal Navy was extensive. Ministry of Supply specifications covering BD issued between 7 April 1949 and 2 June 1954 included 'Blouses and Trousers, Battledress, Blue', to the 1949 pattern described earlier. The next mention is in an Admiralty (Victualling Dept.) Specification of 30 September 1963 covering 'Blouses, Blue Serge, Working Dress, Cadets': 'Blouse with single-breasted collar and lapels, to button three. Cut with centre back and side seams. Fitted with shoulder pads. 2 No. outbreast patch pockets with buttoning flaps. Two-piece sleeves fitted into cuff with button fly-fastening. Bottom of blouse pleated into belt with 4 No. pleats; belt to have 2″ extension left side. 2 No. inside attachment tabs at back.' Buttons for the front and pockets were gilt RN officers' type. A specification from the same source dated 31 January 1964 describes 'Blouses, Blue Serge, Working Dress, Officers' as similar in style to the above except that 'the blouse shall be cut in one piece, i.e. without centre back or side seams'.

The latest specification to come to light, dated 21 and 27 April 1967, applies to blouses and trousers, 'Working Dress for Naval Air Ratings'. The blouse is described as being cut in one piece, with a Prussian—i.e. stand-up—collar, two plain outside pockets with flaps, two inside pockets, and two-piece sleeves 'with a vent fitted into cuff and fly fastening with a button'. The fronts were fly-fastened with four buttons, the bodies being pleated into a belt with a 10in. extension on the left side and a prongless buckle. The trousers had

a map-type pocket on the outside of the left leg and two hip pockets.

Royal Air Force

The RAF, the Commonwealth air forces, and the exile air forces serving with them all adopted BD for both officers and Other Ranks; but it was always considered to be a secondary uniform, termed 'No. 2 Dress' or 'Heavy Duty Dress', the belted service tunic being preferred for ceremonial and for 'walking out'. Although there were trials of a BD suit in RAF grey-blue as early as 1939, it was not until 1942 that its issue became widespread, and 1943 before it became almost universal. The RAF Regiment wore standard Army BD with its own insignia.

The RAF BD was of distinctive pattern. It was worn with the stand-up collar open, exposing blue drill lining and facings, by all ranks: the RAF were jealous of the right to wear shirt collars and ties, granted to WOs and senior NCOs in the early 1930s and to ORs in the late '30s. On the RAF battledress blouse the pocket flaps were copied from those of the service dress tunic, i.e. they were three-pointed rather than tapered to a single central point. All blouse buttons were hidden by flies. The trousers had no map pocket, and the small field dressing pocket was worn high on the left thigh. Photos show examples both with and without the buttons and tabs at the bottom of the

Allied officers in battledress. (Left) A captain of the 13e Demi-Brigade, French Foreign Legion using a sun-compass in Libya, 1942. Very non-regulation dark blue collar patches with gold pipings and green grenade and cypher; gold-on-blue loops of rank braid are worn round the shoulder straps. The képi-cover is pale KD. Interestingly, this officer wears a Sam Browne belt over the blouse, over a khaki sweater, with BD trousers. (Right) General of Brigade Stanislaw Maczek, commander of 1st Polish Armoured Division, inspecting men of his 10th Armoured Brigade. Silver national eagle and general's ranking on black beret; blouse with one black shoulder board bearing Polish ranking, in memory of the black uniforms of the 10th Mechanized Bde. wiped out in 1939; silver-on-crimson national shoulder title, above orange, black and white divisional patch. On the collar points, silver-on-dark blue general's eagle patches. The divisional patch and RAC strip can be seen at right foreground. (Imp. War Mus.)

trouser legs, but they were probably the exception rather than the rule, since very few RAF personnel wore anklets over the trousers. Ranking was worn on the sleeves by non-commissioned ranks and in the form of cloth loops round the base of the shoulder straps by officers.

The RAF No. 2 Dress remained unaltered until after the war, when a style of blouse similar to the 1947 Army pattern with the 'shirt-type' collar was adopted. The pleated pockets had tapered flaps and exposed buttons, as on Army issue. In 1949 the No. 2 Dress Blouse was changed to incorporate a stepped collar with lapels and one-piece, non-buttoning cuffs shaped in a point at the upper edge. There was no central back seam, and the belt tab did not attach to a buckle but was fixed in place by a hook and bar fastening. Unlike earlier

Maj.Gen. Erskine, commanding 7th Armoured Division, inspects men of 8th King's Royal Irish Hussars before D-Day. Far left is a lance-corporal of the Royal Corps of Signals, displaying shoulder title and arm-of-service strip in white and blue. Second from right is a captain of 8th Hussars displaying brass regimental shoulder titles. The Hussar officers wear the regimental green and gold 'tent' hat and red/yellow RAC sleeve strips; all personnel wear the divisional patch. (Lt.Col. George Forty)

issues this blouse had a lining, but not for the sleeves; a hanger was sewn into the back of the collar. The 1949 self-supporting trousers had a waistband with pleats at the top ends of the front creases. There was no field dressing pocket, and no map pocket.

The next mentions found referring to RAF BD are in Specification UK/CIC/1866J of 10 November 1952 ('Heavy Duty Dress Blouses, 1949 Pattern, A.M. Ref No 22N/1-21') and in the specification numbered 1843G of the same date ('Heavy Duty Dress Trousers, 1949 Pattern, A.M. Ref No 22N/22-42'). These specifications, mentioned earlier, covered BD for the Army as well. Subsequent specifications issued up to 2 June 1954 cover BD of Army and Gurkha patterns as well, suggesting standardization of patterns for all Services.

Women's Services

Battledress was first issued to women of the Auxiliary Territorial Service (ATS) in 1941, for those in Mixed Anti-Aircraft Units, for convoy drivers and ambulance drivers. Battledress was later made available to the ATS in overseas theatres, apart from India and the tropics.

The first specification covering 'Blouse, Battledress, Serge, ATS' was issued on 4 September 1941, numbered U/801. It describes a garment of the 1937 style (2 October 1938 amendment); buttons were brass 4-hole style apart from the 'vegetable ivory' ones on the shoulder straps, and the waist belt buckle was the toothed type, of nickel-plated brass. As the neck was worn open over a shirt and tie, an amendment of 24 November 1942 authorized serge facings, and at the same time all buttons became plastic; the 'austerity features' of the male '1940 model' were also incorporated. A single hook and eye was retained at the collar. This pattern remained in force until

16 February 1948, the succeeding model resembling that of male personnel. The BD blouse was worn with either a khaki skirt, or trousers closed by buttons on the left hip, with or without field dressing and map pockets.

Other women's organizations to wear khaki BD included the Queen Alexandra's Royal Army Nursing Corps (until 1962); Women's Transport Service (FANY); Mechanised Transport Corps (until 1947, when the colour changed to bottle green); American Ambulance in Great Britain; Anglo-French Ambulance Corps; Entertainments National Service Association (ENSA); and Navy Army and Air Force Institutes (NAAFI). The Women's Auxiliary Air Force (WAAFs) had battledress from April 1941 when they were first worn on barrage balloon sites; the style closely followed that of the airmen's No. 2 Dress. This similarity continued after the war, the 'Blouse No. 2 (Home) Dress, WRAF' being a scaled-down counterpart of the male blouse apart from the fact that the torso was lined throughout.

Miscellaneous

A large number of organizations contributing to the war effort wore versions of battledress. The Home Guard, formed from the Local Defence Volunteers, wore standard Army BD as they became available (see Plate A3). They received some items of special issue, such as a khaki serge cape for guard duties, brown leather belts and anklets, and special webbing pouches. ARP and Civil Defence workers wore a dark blue version, made from a slightly inferior 'shoddy' or recycled material. War correspondents, welfare organizations such as the Friends' Ambulance and Church Army, and the British Red Cross all wore battledress. Agricultural workers were permitted to purchase coupon-free reconditioned ex-Army BD dyed dark green; and prisoners of war, allowed to work on farms, were issued with BD dyed chocolate brown with a white circular patch cut in to the chest and back.

Associated Items

There is no space in this book for a detailed examination of the other parts of the British serviceman's uniform and equipment in the period covered. The following notes may be of interest,

taken in conjunction with the colour plates.

The types of *headgear* worn by the officers and Other Ranks of the Army, while always subject to tribal variations, fell into a small number of categories. Officers wore the khaki Service Dress cap, with khaki-covered peak, brown leather strap, and badge of regiment, Corps or organization. An alternative at unit level, favoured in the cavalry and the Rifles, was the regimentally-coloured No. 1 Dress cap. These coloured sidecaps were often very striking; e.g. the Hussar pattern was of crimson or scarlet fine cloth with heavy gold piping round the edges and an embroidered regimental badge in bullion wire. Officers of Scots regiments wore the Glengarry bonnet or the tam-o'-shanter—'Balmoral' bonnet—as did their men. Officers of special branches such as the Airborne Forces wore the appropriate berets with regimental badges. After 1943, when the General Service cap was introduced for the troops, officers in the field frequently wore a khaki one-piece beret (sought after by fashion-conscious Other

Monty, Maj.Gen. Erskine (right) and other senior officers confer at the front; Normandy, 1944. Note the freedom of dress adopted by generals! Erskine now wears BD, with his cap badge of rank on the black RAC beret, and highly individual boots. The officer on the left wears a Balmoral and a trench jerkin; his shoulder patch is that of 12 Corps. (Imp. War Mus.)

Ranks willing to risk the wrath from on high!).

Other Ranks of most units wore, from the outset of war, the Field Service cap—the gravity-defying sidecap which could, in theory, be converted at will into a sort of balaclava by folding down the buttoned side-pieces and front peak; this was seldom observed in practice. The brass or white-metal regimental or Corps badge was worn well forward on the left of the crown; simulated-metal plastic badges were widely substituted as the war progressed. In 1943 the General Service cap gradually replaced this. The GS cap was made of several pieces of cloth, with a separate headband, like a Balmoral without the top 'tourie'. A famous departure from the norm was the regimental

version which had been worn since the earliest days of the war by the 'Cherrypickers', the 11th Hussars; this was chocolate-brown with a red band, and was worn without a badge.

Berets of one-piece construction, with a leather rim, were introduced for certain categories of troops. The Royal Tank Regiment had worn a black beret for years, and from 1940 the other regiments of the Royal Armoured Corps were also authorized to wear it with regimental badges; in fact its introduction was extremely patchy, and some cavalry tank regiments were still wearing the FS cap in 1942. The Airborne Forces maroon beret was introduced for use by the Parachute Regiment in 1941, at first with the Army Air Corps cap badge and later with regimental badges. The Commandos received their green beret late in 1942. The Reconnaissance Corps wore khaki berets from 1941 until 1944, when they changed to black. Khaki berets were also worn by 'Motor

Royal Marine Commandos undergoing kit inspection before D-Day; the officer wears a US field jacket. The corporal on the left has '1937 pattern' BD; the round version of the red-on-blue Combined Operations patch is worn between the shoulder title and the ranking. (Imp. War Mus.)

Rifle' battalions in Africa in 1942, in a light shade. In the immediate post-war period the khaki beret replaced the GS cap for general use by most of the Army, being replaced in its turn by the midnight blue beret at the end of the 1940s.

It should be noted that although the peaked Service Dress cap for Other Ranks was officially restricted to Guardsmen and Military Policemen throughout the war, photos show that its use continued in other units in isolated cases.

With the advent of neckties the old collarless khaki flannel *shirts* were phased out, to be replaced by a variety of other patterns until the issue of a standardized pattern in 1950. Many US Army khaki shirts were supplied, presumably under Lease-Lend—and these continued in use alongside British patterns. They were still to be found—and much sought-after—as late as 1969. The first issue *neckties* were of sandy-drill cotton, cheaply made and unpopular. Better-quality woven ties were purchased privately, causing friction with authority until authority finally gave in and approved them as standard issue.

The *webbing equipment* worn by British troops throughout the period covered by this book is covered in detail in Mike Chappell's title in this series, *British Infantry Equipments 1908–1980*, to which readers are referred.

The standard *footwear* was the 'ammunition boot', a heavy black lace-up ankle boot with a leather hob-nailed sole and metal toe and heel plates. Officers had the option, which they usually exercised, of wearing brown boots, often of a pattern without toe-caps.

Applied Insignia

This is a vast subject, too wide and complex to be covered comprehensively in a volume many times this size. All that can be attempted is a listing of the various categories, with occasional examples. Readers should also note the specific subjects of the colour plates.

The insignia which steadily defeated the initial anonymity of khaki battledress during our period fall into the following main categories:

Regimental Cap badges. Shoulder titles; and

Cavalry officers in North-West Europe, 1944–45. At left is a Hussar officer in a gold-piped red sidecap; the red-on-yellow 'Royal Armoured Corps' shoulder title, the black bull on yellow of 11th Armoured Div., and the red/yellow strip are all sewn unusually close together on his sleeve. Centre and right are two officers of 5th (Inniskilling) Dragoon Guards, in khaki SD caps and wearing metal 'collar dogs'. All wear '1937 pattern' BD. (D. Dickson)

occasional use of 'collar dogs'. Shoulder strap identification tabs.

Arm of Service Coloured felt strips worn horizontally on the upper sleeve of the BD blouse.

Formation Patches worn on the upper sleeves to identify Army Groups, Armies, Corps, Divisions, Brigades, and sometimes even individual companies in the case of the RASC.

Rank Insignia worn on the shoulder straps by commissioned ranks, on the arms by Warrant Officers, and in the form of sleeve chevrons by NCOs.

Qualification 'Trade' badges worn on the forearms, indicating special skills or skill at arms. *Brassards* of temporary employment.

Service Length of service and good conduct chevrons, worn point-up on the left forearm. Wound stripes worn on the left forearm.

Decorations Award and campaign ribbons worn on the left breast.

Cap badges do not fall within the scope of this book; interested readers are directed to *Head-Dress Badges of the British Army Vol. II*, by Kipling and King, published by Muller.

Regimental
When war broke out in 1939 most regiments and

corps of the regular Army were wearing brass titles on the ends of the shoulder straps, and/or 'dogs'—small regimental insignia—on the collar points. These were abolished in 1940, but the order was not universally obeyed, and examples may be found in photographs taken throughout the war. The approved replacement was a khaki cloth tab fixed by a loop to the end of the shoulder strap with an abbreviation of the unit title in black letters and numerals; e.g. 'RTR' for Royal Tank Regiment, 'Foresters' for the Sherwood Foresters, '14/20H' for 14th/20th Hussars, etc. Although unpopular for their drabness, these were highly practical; they could be taken off, or moved to other garments, in a moment—advantages not offered by the later sewn-on titles.

As early as 1941 some examples of a coloured title sewn in an arc across the top of the sleeve next to the shoulder seam were to be observed; and by 1943 these were becoming the norm. There were regulation combinations of colours, by arm of service: e.g. white lettering on red for infantry; black or red on Rifle green for Rifles; the Corps title in red on yellow for Royal Armoured Corps units (not worn by the RTR); red on blue for Royal Artillery; blue on red for Royal Engineers; yellow on green for the Reconnaissance Corps; blue 'RAOC' on red for that Corps; white 'RAMC' on dull cherry; and so forth.

Most regiments obeyed the rules, but there are many individual examples of non-standard patterns. Some stuck to their brass titles. Others adopted non-regulation colours. The Yeomanry armoured regiments were particularly high-handed in this respect: the Sussex and Surrey Yeomanry both wore black lettering on yellow titles; the Cheshire Yeomanry wore red regimental titles on yellow; and the County of London Yeomanry wore their nickname, 'Sharpshooters', in yellow on green. Regular cavalry regiments were not immune; the 17th/21st Lancers wore white-on-black '17/21 Lancers' titles. The red-on-yellow 'Royal Armoured Corps' title seems to have been honoured as much in the breech as the observance.

Infantry regiments provide as many examples of unit patterns. The Hampshires wore yellow lettering on black titles. Lt. Col. R. K. May, Curator of the Regimental Museum of The Border Regiment and The King's Own Royal Border Regiment, recalls that the 1st Bn. The Border Regiment never wore the regulation white-on-red titles: 'In 1942, whilst serving in the 1st Airborne Division, [they] wore titles in regimental colours—yellow "Border" on a green background with purple edging. Although frequently told to adhere to the official dress regulations the Battalion continued to wear these titles until 1950, when it was granted the honour of wearing a title with an embroidered glider on it.' The Scots regiments seldom wore standard infantry titles, substituting strips or other shapes of the appropriate tartan cloth—see Plate D. Other tribal affectations, such as the Royal Welch Fusiliers' black rear collar tab, are too numerous to mention.

Arm of Service

Late in 1940 arm-of-service strips were introduced for wearing on the battledress sleeve. These felt strips, 2in. by $\frac{1}{4}$in., were worn above rank chevrons and below formation signs. There were 19 permutations:

Infantry—Scarlet. Where more than one strip was worn, the number of strips indicated the seniority of the brigade within the division, i.e. one strip = senior, two = second senior, etc.

Rifle Regiments—Rifle green

Royal Armoured Corps—Halved yellow (forward) and red

Royal Artillery—Red and blue

Royal Engineers—Blue and red

Royal Army Ordnance Corps—Red, blue, red

Royal Army Service Corps—Yellow and blue

Royal Electrical and Mechanical Engineers—Red, yellow, blue

Royal Corps of Signals—Blue and white

Reconnaissance Corps—Yellow and green

Royal Army Medical Corps—Dull cherry red

Royal Army Chaplains' Dept—Purple

Royal Army Pay Corps—Yellow

Corps of Military Police—Red

Intelligence Corps—Green

Army Education Corps—Cambridge blue

Army Dental Corps—Green and white

Pioneer Corps—Red and green

Army Catering Corps—Grey and yellow

Army Physical Training Corps—Black, red, black

1. Despatch Rider, Royal Signals, 1941
2. Flight Sergeant, RAF, 1942
3. Lance Corporal, Home Guard, 1941

A

1. Officer Cadet, 148th Independent Infantry Brigade, 1942
2. Sergeant, Reconnaissance Corps, 1942
3. Staff Colonel, Northern Command, 1942

B

1. Private, 155th Infantry Brigade, 1943
2. Private, No. 2 Commando, 1943
3. Sergeant, Glider Pilot Regt., 1st Airborne Div., 1944

C

1. Lance Corporal, 2nd Bn. Seaforth Highlanders, 51st Highland Div., 1944
2. Major-General, 52nd Division, 1944
3. Private, 7th/9th Royal Scots, 52nd Div., 1944

D

1. Corporal, Queen's Own Rifles of Canada, 1944
2. Platoon Sergeant, 1st Czech Armd. Bde., 1944
3. Captain, 2nd Bn., King's Royal Rifle Corps, 1943
4. Corporal, RAF, attached XXX Corps, 1944

E

1. Private, 1st Belgian Bde. 'Piron', 1944
2. Major, Belgian 16th Fusilier Bn., 1945
3. Private, Netherlands Bde. 'Prinses Irene', 1944
4. Lieutenant, Polish Carpathian Lancers, 1946

1. Sergeant, Royal Engineers, 50th Div., 1946
2. Police Inspector, Control Commission Germany, 1946
3. Corporal, Royal Marines, 1950s

G

1. Colour Sergeant, 1st Bn. Royal Fusiliers, 1952–3
2. Major, RAMC, 1950
3. Lance Corporal, Gloucestershire Rgt., 1961

The Coldstream Guards had an individual method of identifying battalions by the use of scarlet Roman numerals worn on the upper sleeve, I to V for 1st to 5th Bns.

Formation

The coloured patches worn on both upper sleeves of BD to identify formation stemmed from those introduced during the First World War. Some were resurrected examples, e.g. the famous 'Ever-Open Eye' of the Guards Division, and the broken spur of dismounted yeomanry for 74th Division. Others were of Second World War invention: when the signs were reintroduced in 1940 for all formations (Command HQs, Divisions, Independent Brigade Groups, and Independent Infantry Brigades) commanders nominated their own designs, and the War Office was informed of the choice. The designs were generally fairly simple; after all, they had to be reproduced in cloth, and painted on unit transport and sign-boards. Some designs had regional associations; others were 'puns' on commanders names.

On BD the signs were worn one inch below the shoulder title, above the arm-of-service strip. Materials and methods of production varied according to station and resources. In their most austere form they were colour-printed onto a vulcanised material; others were mechanically embroidered on to coloured felt. More rarely they were hand-woven or hand-embroidered; and there are instances of signs being made up by the troops themselves. Lists of formation signs were classified as Security Documents, and units embarking for overseas had to remove them from uniforms and transport. The Normandy campaign was an exception—the vast troop movement was too obvious to be kept secret. (In practice, every possible combination of use or removal of formation signs and regimental shoulder titles in the front line can be found in wartime photos.)

To list the known formation signs, from GHQ Theatre Commands down to RASC companies, would be quite impossible, and written descriptions are in any case unsatisfactory. There are several good specialist reference books, of which the most readily available is Guido Rosignoli's *Army Badges and Insignia of World War 2* published by Blandford Press, which illustrates several score

of examples in colour. Another useful source is *Heraldry in War* by Lt. Col. Howard Cole. A very few examples may be quoted, however, to under-line the different methods of choosing a formation sign:

HQ Central Mediterranean Force—A white shield with a black border, bearing a black torch with red flames against wavy blue bands. This com-memorates an operation, the 'Torch' landings in French North Africa of November 1942.

Northern Command (Home)—A green apple on a dark blue diamond. The commander was named Adams, and this is a pun on his name—'Adams' Apple'.

Eastern Command (India)—A white horsehead on a black square, the mane being emphasized. This is an even more excruciating pun on the name of the commander, General Sir Mosley Mayne.

XII Corps—Three trees in black and green on a white oval on a black rectangle, the trees being simplified reproductions of an oak, an ash and a thorn. The formation was raised in the South-East of England, the countryside immortalized by Kipling's book *Puck of Pook's Hill*, in which the ancient and mystic properties of these three trees are celebrated.

8th Armoured Division—The word 'GO' in black on a green square. After the highly literary allusion of XII Corps, this is simplicity itself, being taken from a traffic light and the division's motto: 'No Stop; No Caution; Go On.'

13th Division—A black horseshoe on a red square, supposedly chosen to counteract any bad luck attracted by the divisional number.

40th Division—A brown acorn on a white square, commemorating the capture of Bourlon Wood in the First World War by the earlier division of that number.

Regional associations were marked by the 'Drake's Drum' of 45th (Wessex) Division; the red 'Bow Bells' on a blue patch of 47th (London) Division; and Dick Whittington's cat in black on a red square, worn by 56th (London) Division, among many others. The more ancient and dignified martial heraldry of Britain was remembered in the three Saxon seax knives of Essex County Division, taken from that county's arms; and the three yellow lions on a red shield of Force 135, the Channel Islands liberation force, taken from the arms of Richard I, who was also Duke of Normandy.

Rank

The rank insignia of British Army officers are made up of three basic symbols: the star or 'pip', the crown, and the crossed Mameluke sword and baton. In their usual form for use on battledress shoulder straps they were embroidered in white or buff thread with brown details on a coloured backing which showed round the edges; but the smarter versions from the Service Dress tunic, in brass, gilt and enamel, bullion wire embroidery, or black metal were all to be seen on BD at one time or another. The form of 'pip' used by Guards regiments was slightly different from the norm and

Royal Navy battledress blouse in dark blue, with gilt uniform buttons and rank shoulder boards of a commander. (National Maritime Museum)

was individual to the regiment. The crown was the Imperial or King's Crown between the introduction of BD and the accession of Queen Elizabeth in 1953, when it was changed for St Edward's Crown. The Mameluke sabre used in general officers' ranking comes from the fashion for wearing such a sword observed among senior officers in the early 19th century.

The machine-embroidered BD rank insignia were either flat or protruding, made on a cardboard former. The backing was as follows:

Red—General Staff, Royal Artillery, RAOC, Military Police, Pioneer Corps, REME
Scarlet—Infantry, except Rifles
Royal blue—Royal Engineers
Cambridge blue—Army Education Corps
Rifle green, with black ranking—Rifle regiments
Dark green—Light Infantry
Emerald green—Army Dental Corps
Yellow—Royal Armoured Corps, RASC, Royal Army Pay Corps
Dull cherry—RAMC
Beech brown—Auxiliary Territorial Service (ATS)
Purple—Royal Army Chaplains' Dept.
Maroon—Parachute Regiment, Royal Army Veterinary Corps
Grey—Army Catering Corps

The ranking sequence was as follows: One 'pip': 2nd Lieutenant; two 'pips': Lieutenant; three 'pips': Captain. One crown: Major; a crown above one 'pip': Lieutenant-Colonel; a crown above two 'pips': Colonel. A crown above three 'pips' in a triangle: Brigadier. One 'pip' above crossed sabre and baton: Major-General; a crown above sabre and baton: Lieutenant-General; a crown above a 'pip' above crossed sabre and baton: General. Field-Marshals wore a crown above a pair of crossed batons in a gold wreath on a red backing.

On battledress collars senior officers wore red gorget patches (see Plate B3) 2in. long, with a small gilt button at the pointed end, and a line of 'gimp' embroidery down the centre. Substantive colonels on the Staff and brigadiers wore red gimp lines, and general officers gold gimp. From these ranks upwards a red band was worn on the SD cap, and special gold-embroidered cap badges: a lion on a crown for staff colonels and brigadiers, a lion and crown above crossed sabre and baton in a wreath for general officers, and the same but with crossed batons for field-marshals.

With certain exceptions peculiar to unit or Corps, Warrant Officers wore the Royal Coat of Arms (WOs Class I) or a crown within a laurel wreath (WOs Class II) on each forearm. A well-known exception was the beautiful fully-coloured Royal Arms badge worn on the upper sleeves by RSMs of Guards units. In the early war years there was a rank grade of WO Class III, 'Platoon Sergeant Majors', who wore a 'bare' crown. When this grade was abolished, WOs Class II were supposed to revert to the 'bare' crown, leaving the wreathed crown solely for those WOs holding the appointment of Regimental Quartermaster Sergeants. The order was not obeyed with any alacrity, and firm post-war orders were necessary to make it stick!

Non-commissioned officers wore chevrons on each upper arm in a white herringbone braid on khaki backing, point down. One, two and three chevrons identified lance corporals, corporals and sergeants. Sergeants in some Corps wore additional insignia in the 'bend' of the chevrons, e.g. the gun badge of the Royal Artillery, the bursting bomb of the Royal Engineers, and the Mercury figure of the Royal Signals. Depending upon the Corps, a crown was worn above the chevrons by staff sergeants and CQMSs.

Brassards were sometimes worn by Staff officers below the rank of colonel, $3\frac{1}{2}$in. wide on the upper arm, to indicate function:

War Office Staff Halved red above black with gold lion and crown on red part, and lettering in red on black part: e.g. G = General Staff, Q = Quartermaster-General's Dept., TA = Territorial Army Directorate, etc.

HQs Home Forces, BEF and Middle East Halved red over black, plain red part, yellow lettering on black part: e.g. A = Adjutant-General's Dept.

Command HQs Red above black above red in equal parts, red lettering on black part.

Divisional HQs Plain red, black lettering: e.g. O = Ordnance, E = Royal Engineers.

Area, District, Garrison HQs Plain green, black lettering: e.g. GA = Garrison Adjutant.

Brigade HQs Plain blue, black lettering: e.g. BM = Brigade Major.

Men of the Polish Carpathian Lancers (see Plate F4) in the Mediterranean; the use of the 2 Polish Corps patch alone on the sleeve dates the photo to before June 1944. Note also red ribbon above rim of black beret; Independent Carpathian Rifle Brigade badge pinned to left pocket; collar insignia; and mixture of British webbing and leather equipment.

Movement, Embarkation, Transport of Troops Plain white, later with black RTO.

(Brassards in blue with red 'RP' or 'MP' were worn by regimental and Military Police.)

Shoulder strap tabs worn on battledress were very numerous, and defy listing here, even if comprehensive information were available. They dated back to the First World War, when they were used to identify formations from divisions down to company level. The major users in the Second World War were the Royal Tank Regiment, whose many regiments were distinguished by coloured strips of cloth round the end of the shoulder straps: e.g. green for 3 RTR, red and light blue for 5 RTR, red and green for 7 RTR, green/black/green for 25 RTR, etc.

The most common use in other types of unit was to identify companies within a battalion, regiment, depot or training establishment. In the latter case, these coloured cloth loops marked graduation from the despised category of 'recruit', and could be more highly prized than medals! A recorded example of use of shoulder loops within a service battalion is that of 1st Bn. The Border Regiment, who used them to identify individual companies: green, white, red and dark blue for 'A' to 'D' Coys., and light blue and yellow for 'S' and 'HQ' Coys. respectively.

Training establishments—OCTU and Pre-OCTU—used white tabs, and some form of white marking on the headgear, either a band or a patch on the FS cap, or a white disc backing to the badge on the beret.

A further example of embellishment on battle-

Royal Marines sergeant motorcyclist photographed in the late 1950s wearing 1949 BD blouse with khaki serge breeches and calf-length black motorcycle boots. (Royal Marines Museum)

dress is provided by the **lanyard**, which started life as a simple cord to prevent loss of a whistle or knife, but which had developed by the 1940s into a colourful and often intricately-woven decoration without practical purpose. It would be impossible to list the many variations comprehensively; officially-sanctioned lanyards might be researched by laborious study of War Office and Ministry of Defence Clothing Regulations, but there were as many unofficial as official examples.

As a general rule Other Ranks' lanyards were of cotton or rayon woven into a 'drummer's plait', while officers usually sported thick cord lanyards with a woven cotton 'skin'. In some units they were worn exclusively by officers, or officers, WOs and sergeants. An example is the red and green lanyard, worn on the left shoulder, authorised for wear by sergeants and above of the Devonshire Regiment. This was a battle honour, commemorating the stand to the finish of the 2nd Devons at Bois-de-Buttes in 1918, and the subsequent award to the survivors of the Croix de Guerre by the French.

Some regiments or Corps were content to leave the wearing of lanyards to Other Ranks, as in the Royal Artillery. Their white, right-shoulder lanyard was *supposed* to originate in the idea that the last man surviving in a wiped-out battery could link his lanyard with those of his fallen comrades to make a cord long enough to allow him to 'spike' his guns in safety, by blowing up the breeches . . .

The most unusual officer's lanyard was that worn by the Oxfordshire and Buckinghamshire Light Infantry: of medium green colour, it was worn round the neck and separated from a 'Turk's head' below the collar into two cords, one passing outwards into each breast pocket. The reason for this unique configuration is obscure—as are the origins of most lanyards. Very few had the honourable pedigree of the Devons' example. At best they were a way of displaying the traditional colours of the unit, as in the case of the 1st Royal Tank Regiment, who changed from their old red shoulder strap loop to a red lanyard in 1940, to avoid confusion with the orange shoulder strap loop worn by all South African personnel serving overseas.

One of the last types of badge seen on battledress was the **'collar dog'**, which began to proliferate once again at the time of unit amalgamations in the late 1950s. Infantry regiments lost their traditional cap badges at that time, and were made to wear the hated 'Brigade' badges. As a gesture of defiance and in order to display ancient and honourable devices no longer worn on the headgear, 'collar dogs' of regimental patterns were drawn from stores and ordered to be pinned to BD collars. Thus an item which had disappeared as general issue in 1914, and reappeared briefly between the wars only to be banished once more by the introduction of battledress, came back into use just prior to the introduction of No. 2 Dress.

Whatever else may be said about it, there is no denying that battledress made an eminently suitable background for colourful insignia. Veterans recall that as it began to fade at last from the scene, beginning with ACI 89 of 8 March 1961 specifying the issue of one suit of BD for work and one suit of No. 2 Dress for ceremonial and walking-out, the number of different insignia sprouting all over their battledress seemed if anything to increase, in a last blaze of extravagance!

Battledress now survives in Government use in only one respect; as the garb of inmates in HM Prisons. This coincidence would undoubtedly inspire the ingenious sarcasm of the generations of old sweats who suffered inside it in a more honourable service.

Stuart tank crewmen of Indian 7th Light Cavalry, photographed in Burma in 1944, wear the lightweight jungle-green tropical version of the battledress blouse. This was general issue to British troops in this theatre in about 1943, but was not popular and was usually abandoned in favour of shirt-sleeve order. In the Indian Army it saw longer use. Some stocks were still around during the Malayan Emergency of the 1950s. It was made of khaki drill material, dyed green, but the dye was not fast under monsoon conditions, with startling results.

The Plates

With additional research by Mike Chappell and Martin Windrow.

A1: Despatch Rider, Royal Signals; UK, 1941
The Other Ranks' khaki Service Dress cap was officially retained in wartime only by the Guards and the Military Police, but photographs show occasional exceptions to this rule. It was particularly popular with pre-war regular soldiers, who hung on to it as a mark of their superiority over mere 'duration only' civilians in uniform. It is worn here with the Royal Signals cap badge in brass; motoring goggles; the '1937 pattern' battledress blouse worn with Bedford cord breeches; the leather 'trench jerkin'; and chrome-leather gauntlets. The 1937 pattern web belt, pistol case and ammunition pouch are hidden here by the trench jerkin. Note the blue and white Royal Signals arm-of-service strip on the upper arms; the use of two brassards in the same colours for instant recognition of a 'Don-R'; and two Good Conduct chevrons just showing on the left forearm only, indicating more than five years' service. Standard steel helmets were initially worn by motorcyclists, later replaced by a brimless steel type with leather cheek-pieces, and later still by fibre helmets.

A2: Flight Sergeant, Royal Air Force; UK, 1942
This NCO pilot wears the RAF-blue uniform of Field Service cap with brass OR's RAF cap badge; battledress blouse with three-point pocket flaps; and special RAF BD trousers. The blouse was always worn open at the throat, normally over a black tie and light blue shirt collar, here over a silk scarf for flying duties. The albatross badge in

A nice study of an LAC of one of the RAF Servicing Commandos chatting up WAAF medical personnel; France, 1944. These units, whose task was to put captured airfields into operational use with minimum delay, were accordingly well-armed. They wore RAF blue BD with normal rank insignia, and the red-on-dark-blue Combined Operations patch. This LAC seems to display considerable numbers of service service stripes on his forearm—see commentary on Plate D1. The WAAFs display their own version of the blue-grey BD with brass medical caduceus badges on the collars. (Imp. War Mus.)

light-on-dark-blue was worn on both shoulders by all RAF Other Ranks; below it is the brass crown and three light-on-dark-blue chevrons of this rank. The RAF pilot's brevet is worn on the left breast above the ribbon of the Distinguished Flying Medal. The flying boots are the 'escape' type, of which the feet could be removed to simulate civilian shoes when evading capture.

A3: Lance Corporal, Kent Home Guard; UK, 1941
The '1937 pattern' BD is worn with a Field Service cap bearing the badge of the Royal West Kents—a prancing horse over a scroll, in silver. The serge cape is thrown back here to display the equipment and insignia. The white-on-khaki 'Home Guard' title is worn above a black-on-khaki-drill county initial patch, with a battalion number below this. (Some counties had motifs instead of initials; e.g. the Hampshire Home Guard wore a red rose on a black square.) Note respirator bag and shoulder braces from the standard '37 webbing set; the webbing ammunition pouches were peculiar to the Home Guard and were originally designed to hold magazines for the Browning Automatic Rifle. The waist belt is the leather item left over from the 1903 equipment; and note leather anklets, issued to the Home

Guard. The weapon is the P.17 rifle, the red band indicating a .30 cal. weapon of US manufacture. On his left breast this distinguished First World War veteran wears RFC pilot's wings above the ribbons of the VC, MC, and 1915 Star. It was not uncommon to see highly decorated ex-officers of the First World War serving in low ranks of the Home Guard.

B1: Officer Cadet, 148th Independent Infantry Brigade; Wrotham, Kent, 1942
A member of an Officer Cadet Training Unit, about to take a bearing with a prismatic compass. He wears the khaki Field Service cap with the brass cap badge of the 7th Manchesters, and a white 'peak' indicating officer cadet status. The white tabs on the shoulder straps have the same function. The '37 pattern' battledress bears the black-on-khaki formation sign of the brigade above a red infantry arm-of-service strip.

B2: Sergeant, Reconnaissance Corps; UK, 1942
The khaki beret of this Corps—a true beret, not a 'bonnet' like the later GS cap—bears the Corps badge in brass or simulated-brass plastic. (The beret was worn from January 1941 to January 1944, when this organization became part of the Royal Armoured Corps and took the black beret.) The '1937' blouse bears the yellow-on-green Corps shoulder title above the 53rd Division formation sign in red on khaki, and the green and yellow arm-of-service strip below this. His ribbons are the purple and green General Service, at this date indicating pre-war service in Palestine, and the King George VI Coronation Medal. He is operating the 'pressel' switch of a No. 38 wireless set, about to transmit through the throat microphone.

B3: Staff Colonel, Northern Command; UK, 1942
The Service Dress cap bears the red band and gold lion-on-crown badge of this rank. The '1937' blouse was worn open at the throat by all commissioned ranks over a khaki shirt collar and tie; the collar bears scarlet staff tabs, and the shoulder straps woven ranking in white and buff on scarlet —a crown above two 'pips'. Brown leather gloves and swagger stick are typical of commissioned ranks; the field boots are a personal affectation.

The steel helmet is slung on the webbing respirator bag; these were still being carried by all ranks in the UK in 1942. On both sleeves the green apple on blue diamond formation patch of the Command is worn above the red staff strip. Typical medal ribbons for such an officer are shown: DSO, MC and Bar, 'Mons Star', British War Medal 1914–20, Victory Medal with MID clasp/King George V Jubilee, King George VI Coronation, Territorial Decoration, French Croix de Guerre 1914–18 with palm. This selection would be typical for a long-service Territorial promoted in 1939 out of the battalion he was then commanding.

C1: Private, 155th Infantry Brigade; Scotland, 1943
The '1940' BD trousers are the only part of the standard uniform visible. This soldier, on mountain training, wears a khaki ski cap in a material similar to BD serge in place of the standard FS cap. A yellow scarf was worn by men of this division, tucked into the neck of a heavy wool sweater with reinforced elbows and a drawstring neck. Woollen

hose-tops are worn over the trousers, with CWW boots—'Cold Wet Weather', a heavy black boot with a mesh insole and screwed-on rubber cleated soles. The personal equipment in an interesting early rig similar to the 1943 Battle Jerkin, a brown canvas shoulder and waist harness supporting two pouches capable of accommodating Bren gun magazines; it is worn with a mountain rucksack.

It is ironic that the 52nd (Lowland) Division, to which this brigade belonged, never fought in its designated rôle. Although it kept its special clothing—including both white and camouflaged parkas and over-trousers—it was committed to combat in some of the flattest country in Europe, in the Netherlands and west German plateau.

C2: Private, No. 2 Commando; UK, 1943
This Commando left the UK in early summer 1943 and fought in the Mediterranean as part of

RAF Mustang fighter pilots of No. 66 Sqn., 1944, display the RAF blue-grey BD blouse with three-point pocket flaps. (Imp. War Mus.)

Royal Marine officers display the '1949 pattern' BD, and shirtsleeve order. (Left) A lieutenant wearing the green beret, and red-on-dark-blue 'Royal Marines/Commando' title above parachute wings in white and light blue. (Centre) A captain in the dark blue beret with red badge patch (see Plate G3). (Right) The same officer in shirtsleeves, showing the restored belt-loops on the 1949 BD trousers. (Royal Marines Museum)

2nd Special Service Brigade for the rest of the war. The green beret of Commando troops had its origin in November 1942. It is worn here with the silver badge of No. 2 Commando, a dagger point down with the letters 'S-S' divided by the hilt; this was not much seen, as it was officially frowned upon from its first appearance, and regimental badges—or no badge at all—were the norm. The '1940' battledress bears the white-on-dark-blue titles of this Commando at the shoulders, and below them the round version of the Combined Operations patch in red-on-dark-blue: an albatross and a Thompson gun superimposed on an anchor. Below the marksman's badge are two Good Conduct chevrons indicating a pre-war regular, as do the medal ribbons: India General Service 1908–36, the 1936 ribbon for the same decoration, and the General Service ribbon for Palestine 1936–39. The webbing equipment is standard 1937 pattern, and the weapon is the Thompson SMG.

C3: Sergeant, Glider Pilot Regiment, 1st Airborne Division; UK, 1944

The maroon beret of Airborne Forces is worn with the silver Army Air Corps badge. The '1937' BD blouse bears the regimental shoulder title in black on light blue; the blue-on-maroon Pegasus formation sign and 'Airborne' title; and rank chevrons, on both sleeves. The glider pilot's brevet in pale blue, yellow and red is worn on the left breast above the DFM ribbon. The BD trousers have the special enlarged map pocket (and accommodation for a fighting knife in a right seam pocket) developed for airborne troops. This NCO is in the drill position 'For inspection, port pistols'.

D1: Lance Corporal, 2nd Bn. Seaforth Highlanders, 51st Highland Division; UK, early 1944

The '1940' BD blouse is worn with the special uniform items of Scots troops—the tam-o'-shanter or 'Balmoral bonnet', and the kilt in regimental tartan; in this case the tartan is Mackenzie. A patch of the tartan backs the regimental cap badge in silver on the left side of the bonnet; and another strip of it is worn at the top of both sleeves in place of the normal regimental title. (Standard pattern white-on-red name titles for Highland regiments do exist, but are very seldom seen in photographs of wartime personnel; the strip, or other shape, of regimental tartan was almost universal.) Below the red-on-blue 51st Division formation sign is a single red infantry arm-of-service strip; in this division the number of strips indicated the brigade, and 2nd Seaforths served in the senior brigade, 152nd. The two small red reversed chevrons on the lower right sleeve are service chevrons, one for each year served, authorized in February 1944. This makes our NCO an 8th Army veteran, and he wears the Africa Star ribbon. As a Regimental Policeman he wears the standard pattern RP brassard, carries a cane of regimental pattern, and wears white-blancoed belt and white puttee tapes.

D2: Major-General, 52nd (Lowland) Division; Low Countries, 1944

As a former officer of that regiment the General wears the Royal Scots Fusiliers Glengarry bonnet and badge. (General officers enjoyed a good deal of freedom in their choice of headgear; some wore Service Dress caps with red bands and the badge

of their rank, others the cap badges of their rank on their former regimental headgear or on the headgear of their current arm of service, e.g. the black or maroon berets of the Royal Armoured Corps or Airborne Forces; others still retained their full regimental style, as here.) The '1937' pleated, fly-fronted BD blouse has the open collar faced with khaki serge, and the tabs of rank on the collar points. Woven ranking is worn on the shoulder straps on red backing. The divisional formation sign is worn at the top of both sleeves. This officer wears the ribbons of the DSO, MC, and typical First World War campaign and victory ribbons. Officers of all ranks wore brown boots, at their own choice; the webbing pistol set is standard issue.

D3: Private, 7th/9th Royal Scots, 52nd (Lowland) Division; UK, early 1944

The regimental badge is worn on a square of Hunting Stewart tartan on the side of the bonnet. The BD blouse bears, in this regiment, the formation sign at the top of the sleeve, and below it the red infantry strip and another square of tartan. The Good Conduct chevron indicates three years' service. Below it, also on the left arm only, is the gold vertical Wound Stripe; it is backed with a red

Germany, 1945: an officer of the Berkshires and a captain of Royal Artillery wearing the 1st Airborne Div. sign examine an SS tunic. The former wears a khaki beret with the regimental dragon badge embroidered in gold on a red patch; 'collar dogs' are pinned to the immaculately faced lapels of his '1937 pattern' blouse. The gunner has personally-substituted 'woven leather' effect half-ball buttons on his blouse, including the shoulder straps. (Imp. War Mus.)

'enhancing strip', which indicates two or more wounds—unlike their fathers in 1914–18, Tommies of 1939–45 did not wear multiple Wound Stripes. The trews are in Hunting Stewart. Obviously, troops in battle normally wore standard khaki BD trousers instead of the kilt and trews illustrated on this plate, which were reserved for service dress behind the lines or in the UK.

E1: Corporal, Queen's Own Rifles of Canada; France, 1944

An Active Force battalion of this regiment was mobilized on 24 May 1940, and after garrison duty in Newfoundland it went overseas with 8th Brigade, 3rd Canadian Infantry Division. The battalion fought with 3rd Division from Normandy on D-Day to northern Germany on VE-Day. This uniform is preserved in the museum at Arromanches, Normandy.

The battledress and beret are of Canadian manufacture, being of a smoother, greener khaki wool-filled serge than the British type, and of superior styling. The headgear is a true beret, made in one piece, with a black leather rim; it

'1937 pattern' BD worn in February 1945: drummers of the 1st Suffolks parading in the Netherlands wear GS caps, and various ceremonial adornments. (Imp. War Mus.)

bears the regimental cap badge of a silver maple leaf bearing a '2' in a crowned garter over a scroll. The BD is worn over a pale khaki shirt and a black tie. The Military Medal for gallantry and the Canadian Volunteer Service Medal are worn as ribbons on the breast. On both arms the insignia are, top to bottom: title 'Queen's Own Rifles' in red capitals on Rifle green arc; 'Canada' in buff thread capitals on a rectangle of the same khaki as the BD; the plain rectangular patch of French grey cloth—light blue-grey—which was the formation sign of 3rd Division; a scarlet disc bearing a crown over a bugle-horn with '2' in the curl, all in black; and rank chevrons in Rifle green on scarlet.

E2: Platoon Sergeant, 1st Czech Armoured Brigade; France, winter 1944

This brigade of Free Czechs, numbering 247 officers and 4,012 other ranks, landed in France late in August 1944 and served under 1st Canadian Army. They were committed to the prolonged siege of the German garrison of Dunkirk during that winter; main equipment of the tank regiment was the Cromwell.

This NCO wears a British Royal Armoured Corps black beret bearing the silver national cap badge. The shoulder straps of the '1940 pattern' BD blouse have been removed and replaced with Czech shoulder straps of rank in khaki cloth trimmed with cherry red, with a silver button and three half-spherical silver studs. At the top of both sleeves appears a red-on-khaki title 'Czechoslovakia', in capitals within a border. Below this is the national patch used as a formation sign, in bright blue, scarlet and white. (From photographs.)

E3: Captain, 2nd Bn. King's Royal Rifle Corps; Italy, 1943

(Based on a blouse now in the Royal Greenjackets Museum, Winchester.) The regimentally coloured 'No. 1 Dress cap' or sidecap was a popular alternative to the Service Dress cap in the cavalry, the Rifles, and some other units. The KRRC version was entirely in Rifle green. with a small silver bugle-horn badge on a raised scarlet boss, and black buttons. The Canadian-made BD blouse is mainly interesting in having lapel facings added to the opened collar in dark green silk—a splendidly 'regimental' affectation! 2nd KRRC served as the Motor Rifle Battalion (i.e. the integral mobile infantry unit within an armoured brigade) of 4th Armd. Bde. in Italy, returning to the UK in February 1944 after the Sangro River crossing. This captain wears his three 'pips' in black on dark green backing, and the black metal title 'KRRC' on the end of each shoulder strap. The formation sign of 4th Armd. Bde., a black jerboa on a white square, is worn on both sleeves above a Rifles arm-of-service strip. Ribbons are those of the MC, and the Africa Star with 8th Army numeral.

E4: Corporal, Royal Air Force, attached XXX Corps; France, 1944

The '1937 pattern' BD blouse bears a mixture of Army and RAF insignia, indicating a member of one of the small RAF units which accompanied the Army on the ground during the fighting after D-Day. They manned some Auster AOP flights; and served with Air Support Signals Units, the personnel who accompanied forward Army units into action and called down air strikes in support by the circling 'cab ranks' of fighter-bombers. The standard RAF Other Ranks' albatross shoulder badge in light-on-dark-blue is worn above the Army's black and white XXX Corps formation sign, and RAF chevrons of rank, on both sleeves. (From a photograph.)

F1: Private, 1st Belgian Brigade 'Piron'; North-West Europe, 1944

(From a uniform preserved in the museum at Arromanches.) Standard '1940 pattern' BD and 1937 webbing equipment is worn. At the top of the right sleeve a broad strip of ribbon in the national colours of red, yellow and black is sewn above the brigade's formation sign—the Belgian lion mask in yellow on a red cross on a black shield. Below this is the British infantry arm-of-service strip. On the left arm the ribbon in national colours was replaced by the title shown in F2, but the other insignia were repeated as here.

This unit, named after its commander who later rose to command Belgium's post-war army, was the original Free Belgian contingent under arms, based in Britain before the liberation of North-West Europe.

Troopers of the 11th Hussars at Hohne, BAOR, 1962. The regiment formed part of 7th Armoured Brigade, and the old wartime jerboa patch of 7th Armd. Div. is still worn here. Note regimental 'collar dogs' in brass, in the shape of the regimental cap badge; and brass '11H' shoulder titles. (Christopher Rothero)

F2: Major, Belgian 16th Fusilier Battalion; Germany, March 1945

(From the notes and sketches of H. C. Larter Jr of the US Company of Military Historians.) An officer of one of the Fusilier Battalions rather hastily formed, equipped and trained after Belgium's liberation in 1944. He wears a British 'cap GS', the unpopular General Service bonnet which replaced the Field Service cap as the everyday headgear of most British Other Ranks during 1943; the cut-out Belgian rampant lion cap badge in brass is worn above the left eye. The '1937 pattern' BD blouse has a re-tailored collar, open, faced with serge and notched. At the end of each shoulder strap is the brass crossed rifles badge common to all the Fusilier units. On each upper collar point is the gold ranking of a Belgian major: a six-point star above a gold bar divided into a thin above a thick strip. At the top of the left sleeve only is a curved red-on-khaki title, 'Belgium' within a border. At the top of the right sleeve would be the ribbon in national colours worn by F1. This figure would typically wear a pierced brown leather belt from British 1914 leather equipment fitted with brasses and clasp from the 1937 webbing set; and a captured Walther P.38 and holster. There is evidence that the battalion, which served under command of 8th US Tank Destroyer Group in the Remagen Bridgehead, wore British 1914 leather equipment as standard; the usual range of British Army small arms was carried.

F3: Private, Netherlands Brigade 'Prinses Irene'; North-West Europe, 1944

(From a uniform preserved in the museum at Arromanches, Normandy.) The standard British infantryman's clothing and kit for winter fighting —BD, steel helmet worn over a balaclava, and leather jerkin, with '37 webbing worn over all. This Dutchman is differenced only by his sleeve insignia. At the top of both sleeves is a title in orange capitals on a pale khaki drill ground— 'Prinses Irene' within a border. Below it, on the left sleeve only, is the rampant lion of the House of

A last look at battledress, worn here by a staff sergeant, RASC, on the School of Infantry staff. The '1949 pattern' blouse bears yellow-on-blue Corps titles; the School of Infantry patch, halved red-over-blue with a white bayonet; and a marksmanship award, above the brass crown and braid chevrons of this rank. (MOD)

Orange above a reversed arc in the same style reading 'Nederland', both on a khaki patch shaped as illustrated.

This distinguished unit, formed in January 1941 from infantry, engineer and artillery elements of refugee Dutch troops, landed in Normandy in August 1944. They fought through France, Belgium and Holland, being the first troops into the Hague, and later winning further renown in the fighting for the Maas bridgehead.

F4: Lieutenant, Polish Carpathian Lancers; Italy, summer 1946

(From the notes, sketches and photographs kindly provided by K. Barbarski of the Sykorski Institute, London.) This Free Polish tank officer is shown in the full array of insignia worn from June 1946 during the preparation to embark for return to the UK. The black British RAC beret has hanging, knotted tapes; a red tape 2mm wide around the edge immediately above the leather rim; a silver metal Polish national eagle badge, and the two silver stars of this rank. Webbing belt with pistol set, lanyard, and BD trousers are worn in the manner characteristic of this unit; the lanyard always crossed the body, and the web anklets were not worn.

The '1937 pattern' BD blouse, its collar opened and faced with serge, bears a glittering display of insignia and decorations. On each shoulder strap are the two metal stars of rank. On each collar point are the halved blue and red pennons and pinned-on silver crescent and palm trees which identified the Carpathian Lancers. At the top of each sleeve is the title 'Poland' in silver capitals on a crimson arc with rounded ends. On the left sleeve only there appears the silver-on-crimson 'Warsaw mermaid' patch of 2 Polish Corps, above the silver-on-khaki winged, armoured arm and sword insignia of 2nd Polish Armoured Division, above a white strip the same width, similar to a British arm-of-service strip. On the right arm the only insignia worn below the national shoulder title was the British 8th Army formation patch—a dark blue square bearing a white heater shield bearing a gold cross.

High on the left breast, above the medal ribbons, is the silver metal badge of 2 Polish Corps worn at an angle outwards. On the pocket are the badge of the Independent Carpathian Rifle Brigade—Polish eagle, two bayonets rising from a crescent; and the badge of the 2nd 'Warszawska' Armoured Division—a tank through a stirrup below '2'—both in silver metal.

The medal ribbons typical for an officer of this unit and date are displayed: Polish Wound Ribbon with one star/Polish Cross for Valour 1939–45, Polish Army Medal, Polish Cassino Cross, British 1939–45 Star/Africa Star with 8th Army numeral, Italy Star, War Medal, Defence Medal.

The Carpathian Lancers were the armoured recce regiment of 2 Polish Corps until June 1944; in this period they wore on the left sleeve only the Corps patch, and no other insignia on the arms apart from the national titles. In June 1944 the 8th Army patch was added to the right sleeve. After June 1945 the Corps 'mermaid' patch was replaced by the 2nd Armoured Division patch and the white strip, as the unit became the divisional recce regiment; the 8th Army patch was retained on the right. In June 1946 the combination shown here was adopted.

G1: Sergeant, Royal Engineers, 50th Division; Berlin, 1946

We take the basic combination of insignia from a photograph, but have made creative additions! This is an example of a 'tiddly' suit—a battledress heavily modified for walking-out, to match current civilian fashion as far as possible. The headgear is the General Service cap with brass RE badge. The '1940 pattern' BD blouse has the collar widely opened and faced with serge, and is worn over a khaki shirt with contrasting-shade khaki tie. The shoulders have been padded. Triangular gussets have been added to the trouser bottoms to achieve a flared effect. The shoes are polished brown lace-up 'winkle-pickers'. The belt is a late example of 1937 pattern with webbing runners instead of brass. This 'costume', while typical of the spivvier soldier of the day, was highly irregular, and guaranteed to send Warrant Officers into a murderous rage.

Unusually, two formation signs are worn together on the sleeves of the blouse: the black and red circular patch of British troops in Berlin, above the red-on-black 'TT' sign of 50th (Tyne and Tees)

Blouse of a captain of Royal Artillery, 51st (Highland) Division. Red-on-dark-blue shoulder title and divisional formation sign; standard pattern rank 'pips' in off-white with brown details, on a red backing. (Philip Katcher)

Infantry Division. The 'Royal Engineers' shoulder title is in dark-blue-on-red; and this Sapper sergeant wears a brass bursting bomb insignia in the bend of his chevrons. Typical medal ribbons for this rank, formation and date would be: British Empire Medal, 1939–45 Star, Africa Star/Italy Star, France and Germany Star, Defence Medal, War Medal, TA Efficiency Medal.

G2: Inspector of Police, Control Commission; Germany, 1946–47

When the war with Germany came to an end in 1945 the Military Government set up in the British-occupied zones quickly gave way to the Control Commission Germany and Control Commission Austria—'CCG' and 'CCA'. Both service personnel and civilians staffed these commissions, wearing khaki or dark blue battledress with appropriate insignia. A number of British police inspectors were sent out to Germany at this period to help fight the crime which was rampant in a chaotic, starving and divided country overrun by huge numbers of not-always-scrupulous troops with huge stores at their disposal. This officer, clearly wondering whether our natty Sapper has a few ampoules of penicillin in his innocently rolled newspaper, wears khaki BD including the tab-collared blouse of the February 1946 specification; his cap is the normal police type for this rank, of midnight blue material with a black mohair band and black mohair braid edging to the patent leather peak, a black patent chinstrap, and a silver badge. The two silver 'pips' of inspector's rank are worn on each shoulder strap. On both sleeves are shoulder titles in pale blue capitals on

dark blue arcs, 'Police'. Below these are the patches of the Control Commission Germany: a scarlet heater shield with a blue cross, with the linked yellow capitals 'CCG' in the centre, the 'G' being below and between the 'Cs'. (The nickname derived from this insignia was 'Charlie Chaplin's Guards'.) The BD trousers are worn without a belt, loose over black laced shoes. Note white shirt, black tie, black whistle lanyard from left shoulder to pocket, and ribbon of Defence Medal.

G3: Corporal, Royal Marines; UK, 1950s

The Royal Marines beret, of midnight blue with a scarlet backing patch for the brass badge, is worn with '1949 pattern' BD in standard Army khaki, the open collar exposing a khaki shirt and tie of varying shades. The 1937 webbing belt and gaiters are boot-polished black, in the RM fashion, with bright brasses. The unusual shoulder titles on each sleeve are straight rather than arched, with 'Royal Marines' in red-on-dark-blue. Note that in the Marines the herringbone pattern of the rank chevron braid was blancoed-in solid white. The trade badge of a signaller is worn on the left forearm; and this NCO is operating a Field Telephone Type 'L'. The combination of medal ribbons shown would be typical of a young ex-Commando NCO in about 1954, with Far East service in the last year of the Second World War: 1939–45 Star, Pacific Star, War Medal, British Korea Medal/United Nations Korea Medal, Naval General Service Medal (for Malayan service).

H1: Colour Sergeant, 1st Bn. Royal Fusiliers; Korea, 1952–53

The sash and stick identify the Battalion Orderly Sergeant on duty; needless to say, such perfection of uniform would only be attempted when in a camp far from the fighting line. The dark blue beret bears the Fusiliers' brass grenade badge and traditional 'Ordnance' hackle of feathers. The shirt and tie are of contrasting shades. The blouse and trousers of the battledress are of mismatched shades of khaki—almost inevitable—giving a 'sports jacket and flannels' effect. The blouse is that of the 1947 specification, with a broad 'shirt-type' collar, and is tailored very snugly at the waist. The webbing belt is the 1944 pattern. This

This Canadian BD blouse bears the red rectangle patch of 1st Canadian Division below the national title in white on khaki. The label on the inside right hand pocket bears the usual sizing information in British style, and the purple ink stamp '10 OCT 1941'. On the inside left hand pocket are stamps showing a broad arrow enclosed by a large capital 'C'; and the maker's name, 'UNIFORM COMPANY REG'D/1941/ QUEBEC'. (Philip Katcher)

ex-paratrooper wears white and pale blue parachute qualification wings on the right sleeve below the white-on-red 'Royal Fusiliers' title. On both sleeves he wears the formation sign of 1st Commonwealth Division: a pale blue heater shield with a crown in proper colours above the gold capitals 'Commonwealth'. Below this are the brass crown and braid chevrons of his rank. His medal ribbons are typical of this rank and date: Military Medal, 1939–45 Star, Africa Star, Defence Medal, War Medal/General Service Medal (Palestine), British Korea Medal, United Nations Korea Medal.

H2: Major, Royal Army Medical Corps; Scotland, 1950

This elderly quartermaster wears typical working uniform of an officer of this period; the alternative was the Service Dress tunic worn with the Sam Browne belt and with the trousers loose over shoes. The khaki Service Dress cap is worn here with khaki shirt and tie and a battledress tailored to 1949 shape; it is in fact a '1940 pattern' blouse with collar opened, faced with serge and re-cut. (We take these details from this actual surviving blouse.) On the shoulder straps are the rank crowns, in white thread on cherry red; the shoulder titles 'R.A.M.C.' are in the same colours. At the top of each sleeve is the patch of Lowland District, Scottish Command: a scarlet square with a white saltire, with a yellow Scottish rampant lion superimposed centrally. His ribbons tell the story of a quartermaster nearing the end of a 37-year-long Army career which began in 1915 when he was in his teens and included front line service in two World Wars: 1914–15 Star, British War Medal 1914–20, and Victory Medal ('Pip, Squeak and Wilfred'); General Service Medal (Palestine)/ 1939–45 Star, France and Germany Star, Defence Medal, War Medal/King George VI Coronation Medal, Long Service and Good Conduct Medal, Meritorious Service Medal.

H3: Lance Corporal, Gloucestershire Regiment; UK, 1961

The last use of battledress—based on an ancient warrior vividly remembered by the artist, with a few minor amendments. The happily short-lived experiment in reorganizing regiments in regional groups had at this time robbed the Glosters of their

Blouse of '1940 pattern' made by Albion Ltd., Belfast and stamped May 1943. Here it bears the badges of a captain of the Coldstream Guards serving with Guards Armoured Division. Dark blue shield with black and white eye detail, red edging; white-on-red shoulder title; and note particularly the special regimental pattern of rank 'pips', in the form of the Coldstreams' cap star. (Philip Katcher)

cap badge, and the brass dragon badge of the Wessex Group is worn on the midnight blue beret worn by most British infantry regiments. Tradition is preserved by wearing the sphinx badge in the form of 'collar dogs' on the '1949' BD blouse. 'Gloucestershire' titles are worn in white-on-red arcs on each shoulder. Below this on both arms is the US Presidential Citation won by the 'Glorious Glosters' in Korea. Below this, on both sleeves, is the formation sign of 19th Brigade, above the rank chevron. The five Good Conduct chevrons on the left forearm indicate about 27 years' service. The medal ribbons are: 1939–45 Star, Burma Star/ Defence Medal, War Medal, British Korea Medal, UN Korea Medal/Africa General Service Medal

(Kenya), General Service Medal (Cyprus), Long Service and Good Conduct Medal, Meritorious Service Medal. The denim trousers are worn with the serge blouse.

Notes sur les planches en couleur

A1 Officiellement cette casquette n'était portée en temps de guerre que par la police militaire et les régiments de la garde royale, mais les soldats de l'armée régulière d'avant guerre l'arborait souvent. Les brassards bleus et blancs nous permettent de reconnaître les estafettes à motocyclette de ce corps. **A2** Noter la forme particulière des poches sur la version RAF (Armée de l'Air) de la tenue de combat. **A3** Tenue de combat de modèle 1937, portée avec l'insigne des Home Guards; ce vétéran a le brevet de pilote de la première guerre mondiale, et des décorations, dont la Victoria Cross.

B1 Les parements blancs aux épaules et au calot identifie l'élève officier. **B2** Ce corps reçut le béret kaki en 1941. L'insigne visible sur la manche est celui de la 53ème Division. **B3** La casquette à bande rouge et les écussons nous permettent d'identifier un colonel d'état-major; l'insigne sur la manche est celui de la Northern Command.

C1 Cette brigade, qui servit dans la 52ème Division, fût pourvue de vêtements et d'équipements spéciaux pour la montagne; ironiquement, ils furent envoyés au combat en terrain plat, en Hollande. **C2** Ce Commando se battit dans la région méditerranéenne à partir de l'été 1943. Le béret vert des commandos fut mis en circulation à partir de novembre 1942. Noter l'insigne 'Combined Operations' aux manches. **C3** Les pilotes de planeur de la 1ère Division Aéroportée portaient le béret rouge, avec l'insigne Army Air Corps.

D1 Vareuse de tenue de combat, de modèle 1940, portée avec le kilt en tartan aux couleurs du régiment—motif MacKenzie. A la manche, insigne de la 51ème Division; galon d'infanterie rouge; les deux chevrons rouge indiquent deux ans de service; également, brassard spécial et equipement blanc de la police du régiment. **D2** Ancien officier des Royal Scots Fusiliers, ce général a conservé son calot Glengarry. **D3** Pendant la bataille, les troupes écossaises portaient le pantalon de battledress kaki, mais en dehors du combat, elles pouvaient porter le kilt ou trews. Le galon doré sur fond rouge, porté à l'avant-bras gauche, annonce deux blessures, au moins. Ce soldat porte le béret Balmoral.

E1 Battledress verte, de fabrication canadienne; les insignes sur le bras indique la nationalité, et nous informe que ce soldat appartient à la 3ème Division canadienne; les chevrons, avec le petit insigne représentant un cor couronné, sont aux couleurs du régiment. **E2** Uniforme britannique d'unité de chars d'assaut, avec insigne tchèque à le béret, et patte d'épaule tchèque indiquant le rang. **E3** Noter le col à revers 'vert-de-fusil', qui met une touche personnelle. Le calot aux couleurs du régiment, est porté de côté. Sur la manche, insigne de la 4ème Brigade Blindée. **E4** Battledress de l'armée, portée avec insignes de l'armée de l'air, et insigne sur la manche du 30ème corps d'armée.

F1 Le ruban national porté au dessus de l'insigne de la brigade sur la manche est remplacé, sur l'épaule gauche, par l'insigne '*Belgium*' représenté à F2. **F2** 'General Service Cap' et battledress britanniques, avec insignes de rang belges; les fusils croisés sur les pattes d'épaule étaient portés par tous les bataillons des 'Fusiliers'. **F3** L'insigne 'Princesse Irène' se portait sur les deux manches, l'insigne du lion '*Nederland*' sur la manche gauche seulement. **F4** Sur le béret à ruban rouge autour du bord, aigle polonais et insigne de rang; la ruban rouge est particulier à ce régiment. Insignes de col aux couleurs du régiment. L'emblème de sirène sur bouclier cramoisi indique le 2ème Corps d'Armée Polonais; en dessous, on peut voir l'insigne de la 2ème Division Blindée Polonaise. Sur la poitrine sont les insignes en métal argenté du 2ème Corps, la vieille brigade de fusiliers des Carpathes, et la 2ème Division Blindée. L'insigne de la 8ème Armée britannique se porte sur la manche droite à la place des insignes de corps d'armée et de division polonais.

G1 Uniforme 'de permission', amplement personnalisé par le soldat, à l'encontre de tous réglements. **G2** Officier de police civil servant dans la Commission de Contrôle en Allemagne à la fin de la guerre—un mélange d'uniformes de l'armée et de la police. **G3** Béret et insigne d'épaule des Royal Marines; insigne de signaleur sur l'avant-bras gauche.

H1 L'écharpe rouge et la cravache nous permettent d'identifier le sergent d'ordonnance du bataillon en service. La touffe de plume au béret est une particularité du régiment. L'insigne bleu pâle à la manche est celui du 1st Commonwealth Division en Corée. Ceci est le modèle de battledress de 1947. **H2** Battledress de temps de guerre modifié au niveau 'modèle 1949'. A l'épaule, emblème du 'RAMC' (corps médical de l'armée royale) en blanc sur fond rouge cerise. En dessous, insigne sur la manche du Scottish Command, Lowland District. **H3** Un vieux guerrier, les chevrons sur le bras gauche indiquent environ 27 ans de service. Insigne à la casquette des régiments du groupe 'Wessex'; insigne à l'épaule de la 19ème brigade, en dessous du galon bleu de la Presidential Citation américaine obtenue par ce régiment en Corée. Au col de la battledress de modèle 1949 se trouvent les insignes du régiment.

Farbtafeln

A1 Offiziell war diese Mütze nur in Kriegszeiten von der Militär-polizei und der Garde beibehalten worden, jedoch Berufssoldaten vor dem Krieg behielten sie oft zur weiteren Benutzung während des Krieges. Blauweisse Streifen am Ärmel identifizieren die Royal Signals; blauweisse Armbinden lassen den Depeschen-Motorradfahrer dieses Korps erkennen. **A2** Bemerke die besondere Form der Taschen an der RAF Version des battledress. **A3** Battledress im Stil von 1937, mit dem Home Guard Abzeichen getragen; dieser Veteran trägt das Pilotenbrevet des Ersten Weltkrieges und Ordensbänder einschliesslich des Victoria Cross.

B1 Die weissen Streifen an den Schultern und vorne an der Feldmütze lassen einen Offizierskadetten erkennen. **B2** Dieses Korps erhielt die Khaki-Baskenmütze im Jahre 1941. Das Ärmelwappen ist das der 53. Division. **B3** Die mit rotem Band verzierte Mütze und Kragenspiegel lassen einen Stabsoberst erkennen; das Armelwappen identifiziert das Northern Command.

C1 Spezielle Gebirgskleidung und Ausrüstung wurde an diese Brigade ausgegeben, die innerhalb der 52. Division diente; ironischerweise wurden sie jedoch zum Kampf in die flache Ebene von Holland geschickt. **C2** Dieses Commando kämpfte im Mittelmeergebiet vom Sommer 1943 an. Die grüne Baskenmütze der Commandos wurde von November 1942 an und weiterhin ausgegeben. Bemerke das Abzeichen für 'Combined Operations' an seinen Ärmeln. **C3** Lastenseglerpiloten der 1. Luftlande-Division trugen die rote Baskenmütze mit dem Abzeichen des Army Air Corps.

D1 Battledress Bluse im Stil von 1940 getragen mit dem *kilt* des regimentalen tartan—Mackenzie Muster. Ärmelwappen der 51. Division; rote Infanterie-streifen; zwei rote Winkel, die zwei Jahre Dienst in Übersee anzeigen; und das spezielle Armband und Ausrüstung der regimentalen Polizei. **D2** Ein ehemaliger Offizier der Royal Scots Fusiliers, dieser General behält seine Glengarry Schottenmütze. **D3** Während der Schlacht wurden die normalen khakifarbenen battledress Hosen getragen, jedoch ausserhalb des Kampfes konnten schottische Truppen den *kilt* oder die *trews* tragen. Der goldene Streifen auf rotem Hintergrund auf dem linken Vorderarm zeigt zwei oder mehrere Verwundungen an. Hier wird die Balmoral Schottenmütze getragen.

E1 Grünfarbener battledress von kanadischer Herstellung; Ärmelabzeichen zeigen die Nationalität und die 3. kanadische Division an; die Armwinkel mit dem kleinen Waldhornabzeichen sind im regimentalen Stil. **E2** Britische Panzereinheit-Uniform mit tschechischem Mützenabzeichen und tschechischen Schulterrangstreifen. **E3** Bemerke Kragenspiegel in regimentalem 'Jager grün', eine persönliche Affektiertheit. Die Schiffchenmütze des regimentalen Offiziers in grün; Armelabzeichen der 4. Panzer Division. **E4** Army battledress getragen mit den RAF Abzeichen und dem Ärmelabzeichen des 30. Armeekorps von Luftwaffenpersonal, welches zu der Armee an die Front abkommandiert wurde.

F1 Das nationale Band oberhalb des Ärmelabzeichens der Brigade getragen, wurde an der linken Schulter durch das '*Belgium*' Abzeichen, wie gezeigt in F2, ersetzt. **F2** Britische 'General Service cap' und battledress mit belgischen Rangabzeichen; das Abzeichen der gekreuzten Gewehre auf den Schulterklappen wurde von allen Fusilier Bataillonen getragen. **F3** Das 'Prinzessin Irene' Abzeichen wurde an beiden Ärmeln getragen, das 'Nederland' Löwenabzeichen nur links getragen. **F4** Polnischer Adler und Rangabzeichen auf der Baskenmütze, die ein rotes Band um den Rand hat, eine Eigenheit dieses Regiments. Regimentale Kragenabzeichen. Das Seejungfer Abzeichen auf dem karmesinfarbenen Wappen identifiziert das 2. polnische Korps; darunter ist das Abzeichen der 2. polnischen Panzer-Division. Auf der Brust sind Silbermetallabzeichen des 2. Armeekorps; der alten karpatischen Jägerbrigade; und der 2. Panzer-Division. Das Abzeichen der britischen 8. Armee am rechten Ärmel anstelle der des polnischen Korps und Divisions-abzeichen.

G1 'Ausgeh' Uniform, entgegen aller Bestimmungen vom individuellen Soldaten sehr abgeändert. **G2** Ziviler Polizeioffizier mit der Kontroll-Kommission in Deutschland nach dem Ende des Krieges dienend—eine Kombination von Polizei und Armeeuniform. **G3** Baskenmütze und Schulterabzeichen der königlichen Marine-Infanterie; Funkersabzeichen am linken Vorderarm.

H1 Die rote Schärpe und der Stab lassen den Battaillonsunteroffizier vom Dienst erkennen. Der Federbüschel an der Baskenmütze ist eine regimentale Eigenheit. Das hellblaue Ärmelabzeichen ist das des 1st Commonwealth Division in Korea. Dies ist der battledress im Stil von 1947. **H2** Kriegszeiten battledress abgeändert am Kragen zum Stil von 1949. Schulterabzeichen des Sanitätspersonals, 'RAMC' auf kirschrot. Darunter, das Ärmelabzeichen des Scottish Command, Lowland District. **H3** Ein alter Krieger, seine Winkel am linken Vorderarm zeigen ca. 27 jährigen Dienst. Mützenabzeichen der 'Wessex Gruppe' des Regiments; Schulterabzeichen der 19. Brigade, darunter der blaue Streifen des US Presidential Citation, von diesem Regiment in Korea erworben. Regimentale Abzeichen am Kragen des battledress im Stil von 1949 getragen.